STUDY GUIDE to accompany
Dominick Salvatore's

FOURTH EDITION

MICROECONOMICS
Theory and Applications

Prepared by

Mary H. Lesser
Iona College

New York   Oxford
OXFORD UNIVERSITY PRESS
2003

Oxford University Press

Oxford New York
Auckland Bangkok Buenos Aires Cape Town Chennai
Dar es Salaam Delhi Hong Kong Istanbul Karachi Kolkata
Kuala Lumpur Madrid Melbourne Mexico City Mumbai
Nairobi São Paulo Shanghai Taipei Tokyo Toronto

Published by Oxford University Press, Inc.
198 Madison Avenue, New York, New York, 10016
http://www.oup-usa.org

Oxford is a registered trademark of Oxford University Press

ISBN: 0-19-516291-9

Printing number: 9 8 7 6 5 4 3 2 1

Printed in the United States of America
on acid-free paper

CONTENTS

PREFACE

This study guide was written as a companion volume to **MICROECONOMICS: THEORY AND APPLICATIONS**, 4th edition by Dominick Salvatore. It is intended that the guide assist the student in fully comprehending the main text. This is accomplished through several features:

First, **Part I** of each chapter of the guide (except Chapter 1) is a matching column of questions entitled **Review of Concepts from Previous Chapter** which refresh important concepts previously covered.

Second, **Part II** of each chapter of the guide is an **Annotated Chapter Outline** which distills the most important concepts and definitions from the chapter and can be used by the student both as a summary and as a checklist of mastery.

Third, **Part III** of each chapter of the guide, entitled **Key Concepts in this Chapter** is a set of 20 short-answer questions that, taken together, provide a comprehensive review of the chapter material.

Finally, **Part IV** of each chapter of the guide consists of 30 **Multiple-Choice Questions** that provide the student with the ability to self-test.

Answers to all of the above sets of questions are provided in the pages at the end of the guide.

It is hoped that these features will make the guide a useful companion to the text and a valuable review and study aid.

About the author: Dr. Mary H. Lesser is a professor of economics at Iona College, where she has taught for over 20 years. Recognized as a master teacher, Dr. Lesser received the Faculty Speaker of the Year award from Iona College, the Sears Roebuck Award for Excellence in Teaching, and was nominated for CASE U.S. Professors of the Year Program. She has written extensively on pedagogy and critical thinking in teaching economics.

Acknowledgments: The author wishes to thank Dominick Salvatore for the opportunity to write this guide, and for providing the model of excellence in teaching; Stephen McGroarty and Linda Harris of Oxford University Press for their professionalism and collegiality; and her husband, Dr. Thomas Lesser, for his constant support and encouragement.

This guide is dedicated to hundreds of students at Iona College who have been proof of the rewards of teaching.

CHAPTER 1:

INTRODUCTION

1.1 WANTS AND SCARCITY
A. Can Human Wants ever be satisfied?
1. **Human wants**: all goods, services and conditions of life individuals desire
2. **Economic resources**: the inputs for production including land, labor and capital

B. Scarcity: The Pervasive Economic Problem
1. Resources have alternative uses, and are limited in supply. As a result, the amount of goods and services that any society can produce is also limited.
2. Society must choose which commodities to produce and which to sacrifice. In short, society can only satisfy some of its wants.
3. If human wants were limited or resources unlimited there would be no scarcity.
4. Resources change in number, size and type over time, and while this increases the nation's ability to produce goods and services, scarcity remains as long as human wants move ahead of society's ability to satisfy them.

1.2 FUNCTIONS OF AN ECONOMIC SYSTEM
1. **Free-enterprise system**: an economic system in which individuals own property and resources.
2. Faced with the pervasiveness of scarcity, all societies, from the most primitive to the most advanced must determine:
   a. What to produce: refers to which goods and services to produce in what quantities
   b. How to produce: refers to the way resources are organized to produce goods and services that consumers want
   c. For whom to produce: refers to the way output is distributed to society
3. In all but the most primitive societies the economic system must provide for the growth of the nation.
4. **Economic growth**: influenced by government policy to provide incentives to consumers, firms and resource owners
5. An economic system must allocate a given quantity of a commodity over time; this rationing over time is also accomplished by the price system.

1.3 MICROECONOMIC THEORY AND THE PRICE SYSTEM
A. Circular Flow of Economic Activity
1. **Microeconomic theory**: the economic behavior of individual decision makers
2. **Macroeconomic theory**: the total or aggregate level of output and national income

1

3. **Circular flow of economic activity**: the interaction of households and business firms in the markets for goods and services and in the markets for economic resources

B. Determination and Function of Prices

1. If households (firms) wish to purchase more of a commodity (resource) than is available for sale, the price of that commodity (resource) will be bid up until the shortage is eliminated.
2. If households (firms) wish to purchase less of a commodity (resource) than is available for sale, the price of that commodity (resource) will be bid down until the surplus is eliminated.
3. Prices determine which goods are produced and in what quantities, how production is organized, and how output or income is distributed.
4. Microeconomic theory is often called price theory because of the crucial function of prices.

C. What Role for the Government

1. **Mixed economy**: comprises private enterprise and government actions and policies

1.4 THE MARGIN: THE KEY UNIFYING CONCEPT IN MICROECONOMICS

A. The Crucial Importance of the Concept of the Margin in Microeconomics

1. **Marginal benefit**: the extra benefits obtained from an economic decision
2. **Marginal cost**: the extra cost incurred as the result of an economic decision
3. **Concept of the margin**: the key unifying concept in microeconomics
4. **Marginal analysis**: incremental analysis used to maximize or minimize totals
5. **Opportunity cost**: the highest benefit foregone when one chooses one possibility over another

B. Some Clarifications on the Use of the Margin in Microeconomics

1. The maximization of net benefits by marginal analysis does not imply that individuals are merely selfish and does not preclude a certain degree of altruistic behavior.
2. Individuals, firms, and governments seldom have all the information required to maximize net benefits at the margin precisely, yet the concept of optimization at the margin provides the motivation or driving force for most economic actions.
3. Marginal analysis leads to the maximization of individual benefits but not to the maximization of the welfare of society as a whole when private benefits and costs differ from social benefits and costs.
4. When some individuals can be made better off without making someone else worse off, there is a case for government intervention at the margin to improve society's welfare.
5. **Pareto optimum**: when production and consumption can no longer be reorganized so as to improve the welfare of some without at the same time reducing the welfare of others

1.5 SPECIALIZATION, EXCHANGE, AND THE INTERNATIONAL FRAMEWORK OF MICROECONOMICS

A. Specialization and Exchange

1. **Specialization**: refers to the use of labor and other resources in performing those tasks in which each resource is most efficient
2. **Division of labor**: refers to the breaking up of a task into a number of smaller, more specialized tasks and assigning each of these tasks to different workers
3. **Exchange**: when each individual performs only one task in the production of a single commodity, there is a need for her to exchange part of her output for all the other things she wants
4. **Comparative advantage**: a region or nation can specialize in the production of those goods and services in which it is relatively more efficient, and then exchange part of its output for the output of other regions or nations

B. **The International Framework of Microeconomics**
   1. We cannot study microeconomics today without considering the international dimension. The large and growing degree of interdependence of the United States in the world economy makes a closed-economy approach to the study of microeconomics unrealistic.
   2. **Internationalization of economic activity**: globalization of most economic activities in the world today

1.6 MODELS, METHODOLOGY, AND VALUE JUDGMENTS
A. **Models and Methodology**
   1. **Model**: abstracts from the many details surrounding an event and identifies the most important determinants of the event
   2. **Methodology of economics**: to test a theory by the ability to predict logically from internally consistent assumptions
B. **Positive and Normative Economics**
   1. **Positive economics**: studies what is
   2. **Normative economics**: studies what should be

⌘   AT THE FRONTIER   ⌘
DO ECONOMISTS EVER AGREE ON ANYTHING?

There is more agreement among economists than is commonly believed.

PART II: KEY CONCEPTS IN THIS CHAPTER

1. Economics is the science of how individuals deal with: **shortages/scarcity.** *limited resources*
2. We must choose between alternatives because resources are ___*scarce*___.
3. A **theory/fallacy/hypothesis** is a statement that uses critical variables to explain or predict real-world phenomena.
4. Producers and consumer undertake business transactions in ___*markets*___.
5. **Positive/normative** economics is value-free economic analysis.
   Positive/normative economics includes the personal goals and values of the analyst.

6. The branch of economics which studies individual decisions made by economic agents is called microeconomics ✓

7. The highest benefit foregone when one makes a decision is called the (cost) ___. *opportunity costs ?*

8. "Congress should raise the minimum wage" is an example of a normative economic statement.

9. A theory should be rejected if there is an inconsistency between its assumptions and real-world situations. This statement is true/**false.**

10. The topic of the effects of money supply changes on investment is relevant to **macroeconomics/microeconomics.**

11. A **model/theory/hypothesis** is an if-then statement about the relationship between variables which can be subjected to tests.

12. A hypothesis is a theory that has been tested and evidenced to be true. This statement is true/**false.**

13. The situation where production and consumption can no longer be reorganized so as to improve the welfare of some without at the same time reducing the welfare of others is referred to as the Pareto Optimum

14. The internationalization of economic activity is the globalization of most economic activities in the world today.

15. **Macroeconomics/microeconomics** deals with the entire economy.

16. The economic conditions that influence decisions or behavior in an economic theory are referred to as variables.

17. "There is no such thing as a **cheap/free/affordable** lunch" suggests that all goods have an opportunity cost.

18. "Increasing the tax rate on corporate profits will cause the economy to slow down." This statement is pertinent in **microeconomics/macroeconomics** and reflects **positive/normative** economic analysis.

19. A mixed economy is characterized by private enterprise and government actions and policies.

20. Cost benefit analysis is an incremental analysis used to maximize total benefits or minimize total costs. Marginal

---

PART III: MULTIPLE-CHOICE QUESTIONS

D 1. Microeconomics is the study of:
   a. anything small.
   b. the aggregate economy.
   c. the large parts of small things.
   d. the decisions made by individual consumers, producers, and resource owners.

C 2. Macroeconomics deals mainly with:
   a. anything large.
   b. the decisions made by individual consumers, producers, and resource owners.
   c. the aggregate economy.
   d. the small parts of large things.

A 3. When economists study a problem by examining the benefits and costs of small changes in relevant variables, they are using:
   a. the marginal approach to problem solving.
   b. inductive reasoning.
   c. deductive reasoning.
   d. the complete scientific method.

B 4. Positive economics studies:
   a. what ought to be true.
   b. what is.
   c. value judgments.
   d. the correct interpretations of the economy.

D 5. Economic theory:
   a. is a solid body of knowledge agreed upon by all economists.
   b. is not a science.
   c. is limited to predictive statements.
   d. cannot predict the future, but explains the consequences of certain actions.

C 6. Economic models are used:
   a. to apply to a limited number of cases.
   b. to make an exact duplication of the economy.
   c. to predict what is likely to happen under specific circumstances.
   d. to predict the future.

B 7. When economic decisions are made partly by government policies and partly by market forces, the system is called a:
   a. subterranean economy.
   b. mixed economy.
   c. market economy.
   d. command economy.

D 8. "Automobile import quotas should not be used because they result in inefficiencies in the economy." This statement is an example of a:
   a. behavioral assumption.
   b. testable hypothesis.
   c. positive statement.
   d. normative statement.

C 9. Economic resources are best described as:
   a. only natural resources.
   b. financial capital.
   c. labor, land and capital.
   d. only human resources.

10. Which of the following is <u>not</u> true of the prices in an economic system? Prices:
    a. operate only in a free-enterprise system.
    b. give signals to consumers.
    c. can be of many different kinds including rents and interest rates.
    d. operate in mixed economies.

11. "How to produce" refers to:
    a. how output is distributed among members of society.
    b. the way in which resources are organized to produce goods and services.
    c. providing for the growth of the economy over time.
    d. the only rationing mechanism.

12. Which of the following is <u>not</u> addressed by the question "For whom to produce"?
    a. since no society can produce all the goods and services it wants, it must choose which to produce and which not to produce.
    b. output must be distributed to members of the society.
    c. different incomes are earned by the resource owners in the society.
    d. the monetary "votes" held by individuals in the society.

13. "Firms are signaled to produce only those goods and services for which consumers are willing and able to pay a price high enough to cover the cost of production." This statement is the answer to which of the following questions?
    a. How to produce?
    b. For whom to produce?
    c. What to produce?
    d. How to provide for the growth of the economic system?

14. When an economic system must allocate a given quantity of commodity over time, what device is used?
    a. The government must be used.
    b. A lottery is the most efficient device.
    c. A system of "first-come, first-served" is used.
    d. The price system is the device used.

15. When production and consumption can no longer be reorganized so as to improve the welfare of some without at the same time reducing the welfare, of others, society is said to be at:
    a. the equilibrium price and quantity.
    b. Pareto optimum.
    c. partial comparative static equilibrium.
    d. the point of no return.

16. Net benefits from any action or decision will be maximized when:
    a. marginal benefits equal marginal costs.
    b. total benefits are maximized.
    c. marginal costs are minimized.
    d. total benefits equal total costs.

_C_ 17. In the circular flow of economic activity:
   a. governments cannot be considered.
   b. imports and exports balance out.
   c. barter is the means of exchange.
   d. real values flow in one direction and monetary values flow in the other direction.

_B_ 18. The internationalization of economic activity has been:
   a. constant over the last 20 years.
   b. increasing over the last 20 years.
   c. decreasing over the last 20 years.
   d. not important over the last 20 years.

_C_ 19. The problem of scarcity within an economy system could be ignored if:
   a. resources were truly limited.
   b. technological knowledge did not advance.
   c. human wants were limited and not increasing.
   d. human capital decreased.

_A_ 20. In a free-enterprise system:
   a. individuals own property and firms make private economic decisions.
   b. individuals own property and the government owns all factories.
   c. resource owners are told how to use and price their resources.
   d. a planned or mixed economy system must be functioning.

_B_ 21. Economics is:
   a. the only science which studies the behavior of individuals.
   b. the study of the allocation of scarce resources among alternative uses to satisfy human wants.
   c. the study of personal finances.
   d. the study of how unlimited resources are distributed to individuals with limited human wants.

_D_ 22. If households want to purchase less of a commodity than business firms place on the market:
   a. the price of the commodity will fall until the shortage of the commodity disappears.
   b. the price of the commodity will rise until the shortage of the commodity disappears.
   c. the price of the commodity will rise until the surplus of the commodity disappears.
   d. the price of the commodity will fall until the surplus of the commodity disappears.

_A_ 23. If households provide less of a resource or service than business firms want to hire at a given price:
   a. the price of the resource will be bid up until the shortage of the resource is eliminated.

b. the price of the resource will be bid down until the shortage of the resource is eliminated.

c. the price of the resource will be bid up until the surplus of the resource is eliminated.

d. the price of the resource will be bid down until the surplus of the resource is eliminated.

24. Microeconomic theory is often referred to as:
    a. aggregate theory.
    b. the scientific method.
    c. price theory.
    d. the paradigm.

25. A firm producing personal computers had determined that the last unit produced and sold generated less additional revenue than additional cost incurred. The firm should:
    a. shut down.
    b. produce and sell more computers since MC>MR.
    c. produce and sell fewer computers since MR>MC.
    d. produce and sell fewer computers until MR=MC.

26. To the economist, money is not capital because it:
    a. is a medium of exchange.
    b. is a store of value.
    c. facilitates exchange.
    d. does not produce anything.

27. Scarcity is:
    a. the fundamental fact of every society.
    b. overcome because new resources are discovered.
    c. not fundamental to every society because technology always improves.
    d. unimportant because new uses are found for available land and natural resources.

28. In the circular flow of economic activity, rents paid to a resource owner are:
    a. revenue from the firm's viewpoint.
    b. an expense to the firm using the resource.
    c. an expenditure by consumers.
    d. gross receipts from the firm's point of view.

29. According to Milton Friedman, a model should:
    a. be judged by the realism of its assumptions.
    b. be judged by its ability to predict accurately and explain.
    c. use inductive reasoning to generate a testable hypothesis.
    d. use inductive reasoning to arrive at a general conclusion.

D 30. Consumers seek to maximize satisfaction by:
   a. decreasing consumption of a good when MB>MC.
   b. increasing consumption of a good when MB>MC.
   c. increasing consumption of a good when the marginal cost of producing another unit is less than the marginal benefit of selling an additional unit.
   d. increasing consumption of a good when the marginal benefit of consuming it is greater than the marginal opportunity cost of foregoing the consumption of another commodity.

BASIC DEMAND AND SUPPLY ANALYSIS

PART I: REVIEW OF CONCEPTS FROM PREVIOUS CHAPTER

Prior to reading chapter 2, match statements at left with the appropriate concept at right.

_H_ 1. Studies what is
_E_ 2. Globalization of most economic activities in the world
_F_ 3. Individuals own property and resources
_B_ 4. Wants exceed what limited resources can produce
_G_ 5. All other things remaining constant
_C_ 6. Private enterprise and government actions and policies
_D_ 7. Inputs for production including land, labor and capital
_A_ 8. Study of economic behaviors of individual decision makers

a. microeconomics
b. scarcity
c. mixed economy
d. economic resources
e. internationalization of economic activity
f. free-enterprise system
g. ceteris paribus
h. positive economics

PART II: ANNOTATED CHAPTER OUTLINE

2.1 MARKET ANALYSIS
1. **Market:** an institutional arrangement under which buyers and sellers can exchange some quantity of a good or service at a mutually agreeable price. It can be, but need not be, a specific place or location.
2. **Perfectly competitive market:** one in which there are so many buyers and sellers of a product that no one buyer or seller can affect the price of the product, all units of the product are homogeneous (identical), resources are mobile, and knowledge of the market is perfect.

2.2 MARKET DEMAND
A. Demand Schedule and Demand Curve
1. **Market demand schedule:** table showing the quantity of a commodity that consumers are willing and able to purchase over a given period of time at each price of the commodity (everything else held constant)
2. **Law of demand:** inverse price-quantity demanded relationship
3. **Market demand curve:** various alternative price-quantity combinations given by the market demand schedule plotted on a graph

B. Changes in Demand: A demand curve can shift so that more or less of the commodity would be demanded at any commodity price. This could be the result of changes in:
    1. consumers' incomes
    2. consumers' tastes
    3. the price of related commodities
    4. the number of consumers in a market
    5. any other variable held constant in drawing a market demand curve

2.3 MARKET SUPPLY
   A. Supply Schedule and Supply Curve
       1. **Market supply schedule**: table showing the quantity supplied of a commodity at each price for a given period of time
       2. **Market supply curve**: various alternative price-quantity combinations of a supply schedule plotted on a graph
   B. Changes in Supply: shifts in the supply curve due to changes in non-price supply variables such as:
       1. technology
       2. resource prices
       3. weather (for agricultural products)

2.4 WHEN IS A MARKET IN EQUILIBRIUM?
       1. **Equilibrium price**: price at which the quantity demanded of a commodity equals the quantity supplied and the market clears
       2. **Surplus**: quantity supplied exceeds the quantity demanded, which drives the price down
       3. **Shortage**: quantity supplied falls short of the quantity demanded, which drives the price up
       4. **Equilibrium**: condition which, once achieved, tends to persist over time as long as buyers and sellers don't change their behavior

2.5 ADJUSTMENT TO CHANGES IN DEMAND AND SUPPLY: COMPARATIVE STATIC ANALYSIS
Comparative static analysis considers the effect of changes in demand and supply on the equilibrium price and quantity of the commodity.
   A. Adjustment to Changes in Demand: ceteris paribus changes in non-price demand variables cause the entire demand curve to shift
       1. an increase in demand (a rightward shift of the entire demand curve) results both in a higher equilibrium price and a higher equilibrium quantity
       2. a decrease in demand (a leftward shift of the entire demand curve) results both in a lower equilibrium price and a lower equilibrium quantity
   B. Adjustments to Changes in Supply: ceteris paribus changes in non-price supply variables cause the entire supply curve to shift
       1. an increase in supply (a rightward shift of the entire supply curve) results in a lower equilibrium price and a higher equilibrium quantity
       2. a decrease in supply (a leftward shift of the entire supply curve) results in a higher equilibrium price and a lower equilibrium quantity

2.6 DOMESTIC DEMAND AND SUPPLY, IMPORTS, AND PRICES

1. When the domestic price of a commodity is higher than the commodity price abroad, the nation will import the commodity until domestic and foreign prices are equalized (in the absence of trade restrictions and assuming no transportation costs).
2. **Excess demand**: a shortage, quantity demanded greater than quantity supplied
3. **Excess supply**: a surplus, quantity supplied greater than quantity demanded

2.7 INTERFERING WITH VERSUS WORKING THROUGH THE MARKET

1. If the market is allowed to operate without government or other interferences, demand and supply determine the equilibrium price and quantity for each commodity or service.
2. If, on the other hand, the government imposed effective price controls the market would not be allowed to operate and a persistent shortage or surplus would result.
3. In contrast, if the government policy takes the form of working through or within the market (for example, an excise tax), there would be a shift in demand or supply but the market would still determine the equilibrium price and quantity and no persistent shortage or surplus would arise.

⌘ AT THE FRONTIER ⌘
NONCLEARING MARKETS THEORY

The theory postulates that sometimes markets do not clear because economic agents react to both price signals (as in traditional theory) and to quantity signals. One of the main insights of the theory is that disequilibrium in one market can actually create desirable spillover effects in a related market.

PART III: KEY CONCEPTS IN THIS CHAPTER

1. If the quantity demanded exceeds the quantity supplied, then there is a
   shortage .
2. A change in demand is due to changes in _____ demand variables.
3. If the price of a good rises, consumers purchase **more/less/the same amount** of the good, ceteris paribus. Such a phenomenon of change in consumption is a change in **demand/quantity demanded.**
4. The _equilibrium_ price is the price at which the quantity demanded is equal to the quantity supplied.
5. _Comparative Static_ analysis compares one static position to another static situation.
6. The _____ slope of the market supply curve reflects the fact that higher prices must be paid to producers to cover rising marginal costs and thus induce them to supply greater quantities of the commodity.
7. When there is a decrease in supply for a good, ceteris paribus, there will be a temporary _____ at the original equilibrium price with pressure for the price to _____.

8. An introduction of a costly technology is read as a(n) **upward shift of/downward shift of/movement along a** supply curve .

9. An improvement in technology is read as a(n) **upward shift of/downward shift of/movement along a** supply curve.

10. A change in **demand/quantity demanded** causes the market price of a good to change while a price change results in a change in **demand/quantity demanded**.

11. Unlike price controls, an _____ is an example of government policy that is working through or within the market.

12. _____ is a condition which, once achieved, tends to persist over time.

13. Suppose that the U.S. Government imposed quotas on Japanese cars. Such a policy would likely tend to **increase/decrease/not change** the supply of cars in the United States resulting in **an increase/a decrease/no change** in the price of cars in the United States.

14. The law of demand suggests that an increase in the minimum wage rate would likely result in **an increase/a decrease/no change** in the quantity demanded of/demand for unskilled workers thereby **raising/reducing/not changing** the unemployment rate of unskilled workers.

15. "If the price of Coca-Cola increases, then the **quantity demanded of/demand for** Pepsi-Cola would rise/fall". (Assume Coca-Cola and Pepsi-Cola were substitutes.) This is a **positive/normative** statement.

16. Knowing that a Cadillac is a normal good, if the population's income rises then the **demand for/quantity demanded of** Cadillacs will **rise/fall**.

17. When the productivity rates increases in an industry X, the **supply of/quantity supplied of/quantity demanded of/demand for** goods of industry X **rises/declines**.

18. A decline in the price of VCRs will **decrease/increase** the **demand for/quantity demanded of** VCRs thereby causing **a downward shift of /a movement along** the demand curve of movie tickets.

PART IV: MULTIPLE-CHOICE QUESTIONS

D 1. A market:
   a. must be in an identifiable physical location.
   b. is a network of communications between individuals and firms for the purpose of buying and selling.
   c. operates only at the retail level of economic activity.
   d. must involve the exchange of a good.

A 2. The law of demand holds that, ceteris paribus:
   a. price and the quantity demanded are negatively related.
   b. income and demand are positively related.
   c. price and the quantity supplied are negatively related.
   d. taste and the quantity demanded are positively related.

C 3. Changes in the supply of a good may be caused by changes in:
   a. the quantity supplied.
   b. consumer taste for the good.
   c. the level of technology necessary to produce the good.
   d. the price of the good.

D 4. The equilibrium price is the price at which:
   a. the total cost of production is minimized.
   b. the total revenue from sales is maximized.
   c. the average profit per unit is maximized.
   d. the quantity demanded is equal to the quantity supplied.

C 5. When the entire demand curve shifts left, ceteris paribus:
   a. the quantity supplied increases as the price of the good increases.
   b. the quantity demanded increases as the price of the good decreases.
   c. the quantity supplied decreases as the price of the good decreases.
   d. the quantity supplied increases as the price of the good decreases.

D 6. If the quantity demanded is greater than the quantity supplied, then:
   a. the quantity sold is greater than the quantity purchased.
   b. demand is greater than supply.
   c. there is excess supply.
   d. there is excess demand.

   7. When rent control is placed on apartments by a local government:
   a. the market is supplanted or replaced.
   b. working through or within the market is possible.
   c. the resulting rent will be set above the free market.
   d. there will be a surplus of apartments of the type controlled.

Use the following table to answer questions 8 – 12:

Price	$3.00	$2.50	$2.00	$1.50	$1.00
Quantity demanded	16	12	10	8	6
Quantity supplied	6	8	10	11	12

A 8. If price controls were placed on this market with $1.50 as a price ceiling, then:
   a. the excess supply would be 3 units.
   b. there would be pressure for the price to fall to $1.00 due to excess demand.
   c. the excess demand would be 3 units.
   d. there would be pressure for the price to rise to $2.00 due to the surplus.

A 9. The equilibrium:
   a. quantity is 10 and the equilibrium price is $2.00.
   b. price is $2.50 with excess supply of 4 units.
   c. price is $1.50 with excess demand of 3 units.

   d. quantity supplied is 12 units at the price $2.50 and equilibrium quantity demanded is 12 units at price $1.00.

10. If price controls were placed on this market with $2.50 as a price floor, then:
   a. the excess demand would be 4 units.
   b. there would be pressure for the price to rise to $3.00 due to excess supply.
   c. there would be pressure for the price to fall to $1.50 due to the shortage.
   d. the excess supply would be 4 units.

11. As price rises from $1.50 to $2.00, the arc elasticity of demand is:
   a. −0.5.
   b. 0.33.
   c. 0.78.
   d. 0.25.

12. As price falls from $2.50 to $2.00, the arc elasticity of demand is :
   a. 0.25.
   b. 1.00.
   c. 0.82.
   d. 0.5.

13. Comparative static analysis in its simplest form is:
   a. a dynamic analysis tracing variables instantaneously through time.
   b. a snapshot of variables at a single point in time.
   c. comparing one static position to another static position.
   d. a single equilibrium point.

14. A perfectly competitive market is one:
   a. with a single producer.
   b. where no single buyer nor single seller can affect price of the good.
   c. where there are a few large dominant firms with a competitive fringe.
   d. with a single buyer.

15. A change in demand is, ceteris paribus, due to changes in:
   a. the price of the good under consideration.
   b. non-price demand variables.
   c. non-price supply variables.
   d. supply.

16. The market supply curve is:
   a. usually negatively sloped.
   b. always horizontal.
   c. never perpendicular to the horizontal and parallel to the vertical axis.
   d. usually positively sloped.

_A_ 17. The market demand curve is:
  a. usually negatively sloped.
  b. always horizontal.
  c. never perpendicular to the horizontal and parallel to the vertical axis.
  d. usually positively sloped.

_A_ 18. The ceteris paribus assumption is:
  a. holding all factors (other than the one under consideration) constant.
  b. not used in comparative static analysis.
  c. allowing all factors' changes to be calculated and included in the answer.
  d. not a simplifying or restrictive assumption.

19. An increase in supply is:
  a. a rightward shift of the entire supply curve.
  b. a leftward shift of the entire supply curve.
  (c.) an upward movement along a supply curve due to an increase in price.
  d. a downward movement along a supply curve due to a decrease in price.

_A_ 20. The market supply schedule is a table of the quantity supplied and:
  a. price assuming constant all non-price variables on the supply side of the market.
  b. price reflecting an inverse relationship.
  c. the quantity demanded at a series of equilibrium points.
  d. price assuming simultaneous changes in all non-price variables on the demand side of the market.

21. If at a price of $5.00 the quantity demanded is 10 units and the quantity supplied is 25 units, then:
  a. there is pressure for the price to rise above $5.00.
  (b.) the excess supply (a surplus) is 15 units with pressure for price to fall below $5.00.
  c. the excess demand (a shortage) is 15 units.
  d. the government would automatically step in to keep price from falling.

____22. If at a price of $1.25 the quantity demanded is 15 units and the quantity supplied is 5 units, then:
  a. the government would automatically step in to keep price from falling.
  b. there is pressure for the price to fall below $1.25.
  c. the excess supply (a surplus) is 10 units.
  d. the excess demand (a shortage) is 10 units with pressure for price to rise above $1.25.

____23. When there has been an increase in demand for a good, ceteris paribus, there will be:
  a. temporary surplus at the original equilibrium price with pressure for price to fall.
  b. temporary shortage at the original equilibrium price with pressure for price to rise.
  c. new equilibrium price below the original equilibrium price.
  d. decrease in the quantity supplied.

____24. When there has been an decrease in supply of a good, ceteris paribus, there will be a:
    a. temporary surplus at the original equilibrium price with pressure for price to fall.
    b. temporary shortage at the original equilibrium price with pressure for price to rise.
    c. new equilibrium price below the original equilibrium price.
    d. increase in the quantity demanded.

____25. When the domestic price of a U.S. commodity is higher than the commodity price in the world, the:
    a. United States will import the commodity until domestic and foreign prices are equalized.
    b. United States will export the commodity until domestic and foreign prices are equalized.
    c. United States has an excess supply of the commodity.
    d. rest of the world has an excess demand for the commodity.

Use Figure 2-1 to answer questions 26 - 30:

FIGURE 2-1

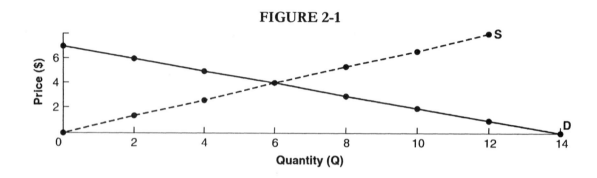

____26. Assume that a government has limited the quantity exchanged of the good under consideration to Q = 4. What would be the highest price consumers would be willing to pay?
    a. $4
    b. $3.40
    c. $5
    d. $7

____27. Assume that a government has limited the quantity exchanged of the good under consideration to Q = 4. What would be the lowest price sellers would be willing to accept to supply that quantity?
    a. $4
    b. $3
    c. $5
    d. $7

___28. A price floor has been placed in the market at P = $6.00. Which of the following is correct?

    a.   There is an excess demand of 6 units.

    b. There is a shortage of 6 units.

    c. The market is cleared at equilibrium.

    d. There is a surplus of 6 units.

___29. If the market were cleared without government intervention, the equilibrium price and quantity would be:

    a.   P = $7, Q = 0

    b.   P = $0, Q = 14

    c.   P = $6, Q = 4

    d.   P = $4, Q = 6

___ 30. Assume that a government has imposed an excise tax of $2 per unit. The new equilibrium price would be:

    a. $4

    b. $5

    c. $6

    d.   None of the above; the market would not reach an equilibrium.

CHAPTER 3:

CONSUMER PREFERENCES AND CHOICE

Prior to reading chapter 3, match statements at left with the appropriate concept at right.

___1. Market price tends to move towards it

___2. Any arrangement of exchange between buyers and sellers

___3. Falling prices cause increased consumption

___4. If consumer preferences vary, consumption decreases

___5. Their changing causes the supply to shift

___6. For these goods consumption rises when income increases

___7. Price being above equilibrium causes this

___8. For these goods consumption rises when income decreases

___9. Price being below equilibrium causes this

___10. Higher price leads to greater production

___11. Higher factor price leads to lower production

a. equilibrium

b. surplus

c. factor prices

d. shortage

e. inferior good

f. normal good

g. change in quantity demanded

h. change in quantity supplied

i. change in demand

j. change in supply

k. market

PART II: ANNOTATED CHAPTER OUTLINE

3.1 UTILITY ANALYSIS

A. Total and Marginal Utility

1. **Utility:** the property of a good that enables it to satisfy human wants

2. **Total utility:** the sum of utility through a specific quantity of consumption

3. **Marginal utility:** the extra utility from consuming one additional unit of a good

4. **Util:** an arbitrary unit of utility

5. **Law of diminishing marginal utility:** the extra utility from consuming a good eventually decreases

B. Cardinal or Ordinal Utility?

1. **Cardinal utility:** an individual can attach specific values or numbers of utils from consuming each quantity of a good or basket of goods

2. **Ordinal utility:** an individual ranks the utilities between various goods or baskets of goods

3.2 CONSUMER'S TASTES: INDIFFERENCE CURVES
A. Indifference Curves—What Do They Show?
1.   **Good:** a commodity that provides utility to consumers
2.   **Bad:** a commodity that provides disutility to consumers
3.   **Indifference curve:** shows the various combinations of two goods which yield equal utility or satisfaction
B. Characteristics of Indifference Curves
1.   Indifference curves do not cross, have a negative slope, and are convex to the origin
C. The Marginal Rate of Substitution
1.   **Marginal rate of substitution (MRS):** the amount of one good an individual is willing to give up for an additional unit of another good while maintaining the same level of satisfaction or remaining on the same indifference curve
2.   The MRS declines as we move down the indifference curve
D. Some Special Types of Indifference Curves
1.   **Neuter:** a good for which the consumer is indifferent between having more or less of it. If good X is a neuter, the indifference curves would be horizontal; if good Y is a neuter, the indifference curves would be vertical.
2.   **Perfect substitutes:** negatively sloped straight line indifference curves (slope is constant)
3.   If indifference curves are concave rather than convex it means that the individual is willing to give up more and more units of good Y for each additional unit of X (the MRS increases).

3.3 INTERNATIONAL CONVERGENCE OF TASTES:
A rapid convergence of tastes is taking place in the world today and has been accelerated by more rapid communications and more frequent travel. This trend has important implications for consumers, producers, and sellers of an increasing number and types of products and services.

3.4 THE CONSUMER'S INCOME AND PRICE CONSTRAINTS: THE BUDGET LINE
A. Definition of the Budget Line
1.   **Budget constraint:** result of limited income and the given prices of goods
2.   **Budget line:** shows the various combinations of two goods a consumer can purchase spending all income at the given prices of the two goods
B. Changes in Income and Prices and the Budget Line
1.   **Shift of budget line:** results from changing consumer income; new budget line will be parallel to the original one and have the same slope
2.   **Rotate budget line:** results from changing the price of a single good (slope changes)

3.5 CONSUMER'S CHOICE
A. Utility Maximization
1.   **Rational consumer:** seeks to maximize utility received by spending income
2.   **Constrained utility maximization:** consumer optimization or consumer equilibrium occurs where the slope of the indifference curve equals the slope

of the budget line and the consumer spends all income (graphically where the indifference curve is tangent to the budget line)

B. Corner Solutions

1. **Corner solutions:** occur when the indifference curve is everywhere flatter or steeper than the budget line or if they are concave rather than convex to the origin. The consumer maximizes utility by spending all income on either good X or good Y.
2. Corner solutions can also result from rationing.

3.6 MARGINAL UTILITY APPROACH TO UTILITY MAXIMIZATION

1. For constrained utility maximization or optimization, the marginal utility of the last dollar spent on X and Y should be the same.
2. This is equivalent to the condition with the indifference curve approach, except for corner solutions.

⌘ AT THE FRONTIER ⌘
THE THEORY OF REVEALED PREFERENCE

A consumer's indifference curves can be derived from observing the actual market behavior of the consumer and without any need to inquire directly about preferences.

PART III: KEY CONCEPTS IN THIS CHAPTER

1. The property of a good that enables it to satisfy human wants is called a **profit/utility.**
2. The additional satisfaction derived from an additional unit of a good or service is called _____ utility.
3. The law of _____ **marginal utility/cost/returns** says that the 4th unit of a good will provide **less/more** satisfaction that the 3rd unit, but **less/more** than the 5th.
4. A model based on an individual's ranking of the utilities from consuming goods is derived from an _____ instead of a cardinal measurement of utility.
5. An increase in the quantity of good A consumed will cause total utility to **increase/decrease** and will cause the marginal utility of A to **increase/decrease**.
6. The _____ gives the different combinations of goods that can be purchased given limited income and the prices of goods.
7. The goal of consumers is to maximize their **total/marginal** utility.
8. The budget line will shift when there is a change in _____.
9. Marginal utility per dollar's worth of expenditure is calculated by dividing the _____ utility from a good by its _____.
10. Suppose Rick receives 100 utils from one more cappuccino, for which he pays $2. The marginal utility per dollar's worth of cappuccino for Rick is _____.
11. Suppose Rick receives 300 utils from a $5 meal. The marginal utility per dollar's worth of the meal for Rick is _____.

12. Based on questions 10 and 11, Rick receives a higher marginal utility per dollar from the **cappuccino/meal**. Hence, if Rick is a utility maximizer, he will buy the **cappuccino/meal**.
13. If a consumer is maximizing utility, the marginal utility per dollar's worth of good A is **less than/equal to/greater than** the marginal utility per dollar's worth of good B.
14. If a consumer is in equilibrium, he or she **is/is not** maximizing his or her utility.
15. Starting from a point of consumer equilibrium, if the price of good A falls, that implies that now the marginal utility per dollar's worth of A is **greater/less than** the marginal utility per dollar's worth of B. As a consequence, the consumer will buy more of good **A/B** and less of good **A/B**, resulting in a **rise/fall** in the marginal utility of B and a **rise/fall** in the marginal utility of A.
16. If a budget line is drawn with good A on the vertical axis and the price of good A increases, the budget line will become **steeper/flatter**.
17. If the indifference curve is horizontal or vertical it means that good X or good Y are **neuters/perfect substitutes**.
18. Indifference curves cannot **intersect/have a negative slope**.
19. The marginal rate of substitution is the ratio of the **prices/marginal utilities/quantities of two goods**.
20. The point of consumer optimization is shown graphically as the point where the budget line and the indifference curve **intersect/are tangent**.

PART IV: MULTIPLE-CHOICE QUESTIONS

____1. Utility is:
   a. water, gas and electricity.
   b. the basis of supply analysis.
   c. the property of a good that enables it to satisfy human wants.
   d. producing a good and making it available in a market.

____2. When less of a good is preferred to more of the good, the good is called:
   a. a bad.
   b. a good.
   c. inferior.
   d. superior.

____3. The marginal rate of substitution (MRS) is the:
   a. slope of the demand curve.
   b. slope of the demand curve multiplied by the price-quantity ratio.
   c. slope of the supply curve.
   d. amount of one good that is given up for an additional unit of another good at a constant level of utility.

____4. As the world becomes one global market:
- a. the living styles of middle-class people are becoming more dissimilar.
- b. the types of products and services decrease.
- c. cross fertilization of cultures and convergence of tastes can be expected.
- d. national economic isolation will increase.

____5. Since consumers have limited income at given prices, they are said to:
- a. face a cost function.
- b. face a budget constraint.
- c. have limited wants.
- d. operate on a production possibilities frontier.

____6. The rational consumer:
- a. seeks to maximize the utility received from spending income.
- b. move up the budget line.
- c. has a utility map with straight line indifference curves.
- d. has a marginal rate of substitution greater than one.

____7. When indifference curves are everywhere flatter than the budget line there is:
- a. a corner solution on the horizontal axis.
- b. a tangency solution in the positive space or Q_x and Q_y.
- c. no solution.
- d. a corner solution on the vertical axis.

____8. If the total utility associated with the first 3 units of a good is $TU_1 = 15$, $TU_2 = 19$, and $TU_3 = 22$, then:
- a. the average utility associated with $Q_1 = 15$.
- b. the marginal utility associated with changing from Q_2 to Q_3 is 3.
- c. the total utility associated with Q_4 must be less than 22 according to the law of diminishing marginal utility.
- d. ordinal utility cannot apply in this case.

____9. In indifference curve analysis, if we assume that a commodity is a good rather than a bad, the:
- a. consumer must buy the good.
- b. consumer is never satisfied with the commodity (i.e., more is preferred to less).
- c. two indifference curves cross.
- d. two budget lines cross.

____10. An indifference curve shows the:
- a. various combinations of two goods that give the consumer equal utility.
- b. price-quantity combinations that reflect an inverse relationship.
- c. price-quantity combinations that reflect a positive relationship.
- d. various combinations of two goods that the consumer can purchase by spending all income at given prices.

____11. If a change in Q_x of 2 units results in a change in marginal utility (MU_x) of 15 when the change in Q_y is -3, and assuming that the total utility is constant, then the change in marginal utility associated with good y (MU_y) is:
   a.   10.
   b.   30.
   c.   -10.
   d.   Not possible to calculate assuming cardinal utility.

____12. Assuming that good x is on the horizontal axis and good y is on the vertical axis, good x is neuter when the:
   a.   marginal rate of substitution of good x for good y (MRS_{xy}) is equal to infinity.
   b.   indifference curve is perpendicular to the horizontal axis and parallel to the vertical axis.
   c. MRS_{xy} is equal to zero.
   d.   indifference curve is concave.

If the quantity of good x (Q_x) is on the horizontal axis and the quantity of good y (Q_y) is on the vertical axis, and assuming that the consumer budget is exhausted, income (I) of $100, price of good y ($P_y$) equals $5, price of good x ($P_x$) equals $20 and Q_x purchased is 2, answer questions 13 - 17:

____13. What is the Q_y purchased, *ceteris paribus?*
   a.   2
   b.   5
   c.   20
   d.   12

____14. What would happen to the budget line if P_x falls to $10, *ceteris paribus?*
   a.   It would shift outward.
   b.   It would shift inward.
   c.   It would rotate clockwise with new horizontal intercept of 10.
   d.   It would rotate counterclockwise with new horizontal intercept of 10.

____15. What would happen to the budget line if income (I) falls to $50, *ceteris paribus?*
   a.   It would rotate clockwise.
   b.   It would rotate counterclockwise.
   c.   It would shift inward with vertical intercept of 10 and a horizontal intercept of 2.5.
   d.   It would shift outward with vertical intercept of 10 and a horizontal intercept of 2.5.

____16. What is the Q_y if P_x falls to zero, *ceteris paribus?*
   a.   20
   b.   12
   c.   2
   d.   infinity

___17. What is the Q_x if P_y falls to zero, *ceteris paribus?*
    a. 2
    b. 5
    c. 20
    d. 12

___18. Constrained utility maximization occurs when:
    a. the budget line crosses the indifference curve.
    b. the slope of the budget line is equal to the slope of the indifference curve.
    c. the budget is not exhausted on expenditures for the goods under consideration.
    d. borrowing is necessary to purchase the goods under consideration.

___19. If utility were cardinally measurable, consumer equilibrium would be achieved when:
    a. total utility is increasing at an increasing rate.
    b. marginal utility is at a maximum.
    c. average utility is at a maximum.
    d. the marginal utility per dollar spent on each good is equal.

___20. If the assumptions in question 19 were correct, consumer optimization also occurs when the:
    a. marginal rate of substitution of good x for good y equals the ratio of marginal utility of good x over the marginal utility of good y.
    b. marginal rate of substitution of good x for good y equals the ratio of marginal utility of good y over the marginal utility of good x.
    c. marginal rate of substitution of good x for good y equals the ratio of price of good x over the price of good y.
    d. marginal rate of substitution of good x for good y equals the marginal rate of substitution of good y for good x.

___21. The saturation point is when:
    a. consuming another unit of the good x leaves total utility (TU_x) unchanged.
    b. marginal utility (MU_x) is at a maximum.
    c. MU_x per dollar is equal to the MU_y per dollar.
    d. TU_x is increasing at an increasing rate.

___22. The law of diminishing marginal utility is indicated by:
    a. an upward sloped supply curve.
    b. continuously rising total utility.
    c. the downward-to-the-right inclination of the marginal utility curve.
    d. consumers preferring more of a good than less.

___23. If either good x or good y is an economic bad, then the indifference curve:
    a. approaches the x axis and y axis but does not touch either.
    b. is a straight line which crosses both the x and y axes.
    c. is positively sloped.
    d. must cross other indifference curves in the indifference map.

_____24. If good x is on the horizontal axis and good y is on the vertical axis, the marginal rate of substitution of good x for good y (MRS_{xy}) diminishes as one slides down an indifference curve if:
   a.   the slope of the demand curve is positive over the same range of good x.
   b.   the MRS_{yx} diminishes as one moves in an upward direction on the same range.
   c.   The MRS_{xy} is equal to the ratio of prices, P_x/P_y.
   d. MRS_{xy} is equal to the ratio of marginal utilities, MU_y/MU_x.

_____25. If good x is on the horizontal axis and good y is on the vertical axis, the marginal rate of substitution of good x for good y (MRS_{xy}) increases as one slides down an indifference curve if:
   a.   the point of tangency with a budget line will result in a stable equilibrium.
   b.   there will be equilibrium where the indifference curve crosses a budget line.
   c.   the indifference curve will be positively sloped.
   d.   there will be a corner solution.

Use Figure 3-1 to answer questions 26 - 30:

FIGURE 3-1

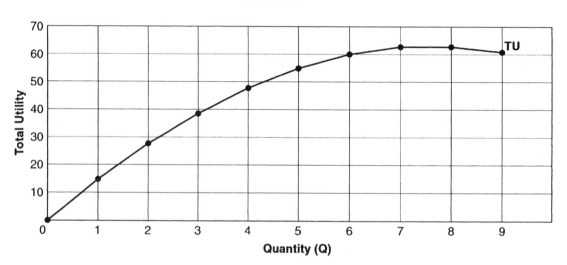

_____26. The point of saturation is between quantities:
   a.   8 and 9
   b.   0 and 4
   c.   4 and 7
   d.   7 and 8

_____27. The marginal utility of good x (MU_x) is negative between quantities:
   a.   7 and 8
   b.   8 and 9
   c.   0 and 4
   d.   4 and 7

___28. Between quantities 0 and 7, the total utility curve is:
   a. reflecting the law of increasing marginal utility (MU_x), but does not from quantities 7 through 9.
   b. increasing at an increasing rate, and decreasing at a decreasing rate from quantities 7 through 9.
   c. reflecting the law of diminishing marginal utility (MU_x), as it also does from quantities 7 through 9.
   d. reflecting constant marginal utility (MU_x).

___29. Where will the consumer be in equilibrium?
   a. Between quantities 7 and 8 since the marginal utility (MU_x) is zero.
   b. At quantity 8 since the marginal utility (MU_x) between quantities 8 and 9 are negative.
   c. At quantity 7 since the saturation point is between quantities 7 and 8.
   d. Cannot be determined from the information provided; one must have information on the marginal utilities per dollar of the two goods to determine equilibrium.

___30. How would the total utility (TU_x) curve presented be different if at least part of the marginal utility (MU_x) curve were positively sloped?
   a. It would not need to be different because MU_x is negative between quantities 8 and 9.
   b. The TU_x curve increases at an increasing rate between quantities 0 and 3.
   c. It would not need to be different because MU_x is positive between quantities 0 and 7.
   d. It would not need to be different because MU_x diminishes throughout.

CHAPTER 4:

CONSUMER BEHAVIOR AND INDIVIDUAL DEMAND

PART I: REVIEW OF CONCEPTS FROM PREVIOUS CHAPTER

Prior to reading chapter 4, match statements at left with the appropriate concept at right.

____1. Incremental or additional
____2. Change in consumption resulting from a change in price
____3. Less is consumed of it as real income rises
____4. No tendency to change away from this situation
____5. Slope of budget line
____6. Slope of indifference curve
____7. A lower price corresponds to a higher quantity demanded
____8. Less is consumed of it as real income declines
____9. Consumer equilibrium
___10. Satisfaction or happiness

a. normal good
b. inferior good
c. utility
d. change in quantity demanded
e. marginal
f. negative ratio of goods' prices
g. negative ratio of marginal utilities
h. law of demand
i. ratio of prices = ratio of marginal utilities
j. equilibrium

PART II: ANNOTATED CHAPTER OUTLINE

4.1 CHANGES IN INCOME AND THE ENGEL CURVE
A. Income-Consumption Curve and Engel Curve
   1. **Income-consumption curve**: locus of consumer optimum points resulting when only the consumer's income varies
   2. **Engel curve**: shows the amount of a good that the consumer would purchase per unit of time at various income levels
B. Normal and Inferior Goods
   1. **Normal good**: one of which the consumer purchases more when income increases
   2. **Inferior good**: one of which the consumer purchases less when income increases

4.2 CHANGES IN PRICE AND THE INDIVIDUAL DEMAND CURVE

1. **Price-consumption curve**: locus of consumer optimum points resulting when only the price of good X varies
2. **Individual demand curve**: amounts of the good that the consumer would purchase per unit of time at various prices, holding everything else constant

4.3 SUBSTITUTION AND INCOME EFFECTS
A. How are the Substitution and Income Effects Separated?
1. **Substitution effect**: change in the quantity demanded of a good as the price of that good changes due to changes in relative prices
2. **Income effect**: change in the quantity demanded of a good as the price of that good changes due to changes in real income
B. Substitution and Income Effects for Inferior Goods
1. For normal goods the substitution and income effects of a price decline are both positive and reinforce each other, leading to a greater quantity purchased of the good.
2. When the good is inferior, the income effect moves in the opposite direction from the substitution effect, but since the substitution effect is usually stronger than the income effect the quantity demanded still increases when the price falls.
3. A Giffen good is an inferior good for which the demand curve is positively sloped; this occurs because the income effect is larger (and has the opposite sign) than the substitution effect. Thus as the price falls less of the good is purchased.

4.4 SUBSTITUTION BETWEEN DOMESTIC AND FOREIGN GOODS
1. Substitution is at an all-time high in the world today and is expected to continue to increase sharply.
2. It is due to decreases in transportation cost, the information revolution, global advertising, increased international travel and rapid convergence of tastes internationally.

4.5 SOME APPLICATIONS OF INDIFFERENCE CURVE ANALYSIS
A. Is a Cash Subsidy Better than Food Stamps?
1. **Federal food stamp program**: low-income families receiving free food stamps may receive a higher level of utility from a cash grant of equal value.
B. Consumer Surplus Measures Unpaid Benefits
1. **Consumer surplus**: difference between what a consumer is willing to pay for a good and what the consumer actually pays
2. **Water-diamond paradox**: why is water, which is essential for life, so cheap, while diamonds, which are not essential are so expensive? The explanation is that water is so plentiful, so the last unit has very little utility. Diamonds, however, are scarce, so the utility and price of the last unit are very high.
C. The Benefits from Exchange
1. **Edgeworth box diagram**: a method used to show the indifference curves for two individuals each consuming the same two goods and the path to equilibrium through mutually beneficial exchange

⌘ AT THE FRONTIER ⌘
THE CHARACTERISTICS APPROACH TO CONSUMER THEORY

The approach postulates that consumers demand a good because of its characteristics, properties, or attributes of the good, and it is these characteristics that give rise to utility.

PART III: KEY CONCEPTS IN THIS CHAPTER

1. When the consumer has spent all his or her income and the marginal utilities per dollar spent on each good purchased are equal, the consumer is said to be _____.

2. The _____ measures the increase in the quantity purchased of a good resulting only from the increase in real income that accompanies a price decline.

3. The difference between the price buyers pay for a good and the maximum price they would have paid for the good is _____.

4. The demand curve for good X is given by $Q_{dx} = 12 - P_x$. If the $P_{x1} = 6$, then $Q_{dx1} = 6$, whereas if $P_{x2} = 12$ then $Q_{dx2} = 0$. Consumer surplus is equal to _____.

5. The demand curve for good X is given by $Q_{dx} = 8 - P_x$. If the $P_{x1} = 3$, then $Q_{dx1} = 5$, whereas if $P_{x2} = 8$ then $Q_{dx2} = 0$. Consumer surplus is equal to _____.

6. In the water-diamond paradox, the marginal utility of water is _____ than that of diamonds. The total utility of water is _____ than that of diamonds.

7. The water-diamond paradox suggests that the market price of a good depends on the _____ utility it provides.

8. An _____ is used to study the coordination of consumption and utility analysis for two individuals each consuming the same two goods, X and Y.

9. An income-consumption curve with a positive slope results in a positively sloped Engel curve reflecting a _____ good.

10. The _____ effect of a price decline is usually positive, leading a consumer to purchase more of the good whose price has fallen.

11. The marginal rate of substitution of good X for good y (MRS_{XY}) is equal to the price of good X (P_X) divided by the price of good Y (P_Y) at every point on the _____ curve.

12. The _____ curve shows the amounts of a good the consumer would purchase per unit of time at various income levels.

13. The locus of consumer optimum points resulting when only the consumer's income varies is the _____ curve.

14. The locus of consumer optimum points resulting when only the price of good X varies is the _____ curve.

15. The individual's demand curve for a good is usually _____ sloped.

16. The amount of a good that the consumer would purchase per unit of time at various alternative prices while holding everything else constant is the individual's _____ curve.

17. When the demand for an inferior good is positively sloped because the income effect is larger (and has the opposite sign) than the substitution effect, such a good is called a(n) _____ good.

18. The slope of the demand curve for an inferior good (but not a Giffen good) is _____.

19. Inferior goods are characterized by a _____ income effect: as income increases, the quantity demanded _____ or as income decreases, the quantity demanded _____.

20. The _____ diagram is a method used to show the indifference curves for two individuals each consuming the same two goods and the path to equilibrium through mutually beneficial exchange.

PART IV: MULTIPLE-CHOICE QUESTIONS

____1. The income-consumption curve is:
   a. used to derive a demand curve.
   b. the locus of consumer optimum points resulting when only the price of good X varies.
   c. reveals the substitution effect and income effect.
   d. the locus of consumer optimum points resulting when only the consumer's income varies.

____2. The price-consumption curve is:
   a. the locus of consumer optimum points resulting when only the consumer's income varies.
   b. used to derive an Engel curve.
   c. the locus of consumer optimum points resulting when only the price of good X varies.
   d. is not used to determine if a good is a Giffen good.

____3. The substitution effect results from:
   a. the change in money income.
   b. the relative reduction in the price of the good under consideration.
   c. the change in real income.
   d. a shift in the Engel curve.

____4. Which of the following is not a reason for the substitution between domestic and foreign goods and services reaching an all-time high?
   a. the expansion of Giffen goods internationally
   b. the rapid convergence of tastes internationally
   c. the decrease in transportation costs to very low levels for most products
   d. global advertising campaigns by multinational corporations

___5. Consumer surplus is the:
   a. difference between what a consumer is willing to pay for a good and what he or she actually pays.
   b. area under a demand curve.
   c. area under a supply curve.
   d. difference between what a producer receives for a good and the minimum amount necessary to bring the good into production.

___6. Providing poor families with food stamps versus a cash grant of the same value:
   a. always results in higher utility associated with food stamps.
   b. always results in lower utility because families prefer cash.
   c. affects families depending on their indifference map.
   d. is unimportant since the cash grant may be traded for food stamps or the food stamps traded for cash.

___7. When the price of an inferior good falls and the positive substitution effect is smaller than the negative income effect, then the:
   a. demand curve for the inferior good has a negative slope.
   b. demand curve for this Giffen good has a positive slope.
   c. net effect is positive.
   d. indifference map must have indifference curves with positive slopes.

___8. The income effect results from:
   a. a change in money income.
   b. a relative reduction in the price of the good under consideration.
   c. a change in real income.
   d. shifts in the income-consumption curve.

___9. If the price of good X falls and the consumer buys less of good X, then the good must be:
   a. normal.
   b. inferior.
   c. a Giffen good.
   d. either inferior or a Giffen good.

___10. An individual's demand curve for the good X shows:
   a. the marginal utility associated with each level of Q_X.
   b. the consumer surplus as the area under the curve.
   c. a positive relationship with price changes, ceteris paribus.
   d. the amount of X (Q_x) that the consumer would purchase per unit of time at various prices, ceteris paribus.

___11. As the income of an individual increases from $150 to $300 per week, the consumer purchases:
   a. less of a normal good.
   b. the good X (Q_x) in a pattern reflected on a positively sloped Engel curve for an inferior good.

   c. the good X (Q_X) in a pattern reflected on a positive substitution and a positive income effect for an inferior good.

   d. less of X in a pattern reflected on a negatively sloped Engel curve for an inferior good.

___12. An Engel curve shows:

   a. the amount of good X (Q_X) the consumer would purchase per unit of time at various income levels.

   b. the locus of consumer optimum points resulting when only the price of good X varies.

   c. the locus of consumer optimum points between Q_X and another good Y resulting when only the consumer's income varies.

   d. the income and substitution effects.

___13. Under the federal food stamp program, low-income families receive free food stamps, which they can:

   a. use only to purchase food.

   b. trade for cash.

   c. use to purchase anything in any store.

   d. trade for housing vouchers.

___14. If good X (Q_X) can be purchased in infinitesimally small units and a straight-line demand curve with a y-axis intercept of P_Y, the consumer surplus is:

   a. the area under the demand curve.

   b. equal to Q_X times P_X.

   c. one-half the area of Q_X [P_Y-P_X]

   d. the area under P_X above the supply curve.

___15. The water-diamond paradox is:

   a. the idea that Giffen goods are rare.

   b. an analysis of inferior goods.

   c. solved when price is associated with marginal utility.

   d. solved when price is associated with total utility.

___16. When individual A's indifference diagram is rotated 180 degrees and superimposed on individual B's indifference diagram, the two diagrams:

   a. form an Engel curve.

   b. form an Edgeworth box diagram.

   c. derive an income-consumption curve and box.

   d. derive a price-consumption curve and box.

___17. In an Edgeworth box diagram representing the indifference curves of individuals A and B, mutually beneficial exchange will take place until:

   a. marginal utility A is equal to marginal utility B.

   b. indifference curves from each individual cross.

   c. one individual has all of the goods available.

   d. the marginal rate of substitution of good X for good Y is the same for each individual.

___18. One characteristic of an Engel curve is the:
a. substitution effect.
b. inverse relationship between price and quantity demanded.
c. marginal rate of substitution of good X for good Y (MRS_{XY}) is equal to the marginal utility of good Y (MU_Y) divided by the marginal utility of good X (MU_X) at every point on the curve.
d. marginal rate of substitution of good X for good Y (MRS_{XY}) is equal to the price of good X (P_X) divided by the price of good Y(P_Y) at every point on the curve.

___19. If an income-consumption curve is drawn from two consumer equilibrium points with the coordinates [Q_{y1} = 12, Q_{x1} = 2] and [Q_{y2} = 7, Q_{x2} = 4], then it can be concluded that the:
a. Engel curve has negative slope reflecting an inferior good.
b. Engel curve has positive slope reflecting a normal good.
c. Price-consumption curve will indicate a Giffen good.
d. Income-consumption curve has a positive slope.

___20. If a price-consumption curve is drawn from two consumer equilibrium points with the coordinates [Q_{y1} = 12, Q_{x1} = 2] and [Q_{y2} = 7, Q_{x2} = 4], then it can be concluded that the demand curve is:
a. negatively sloped.
b. positively sloped.
c. vertical.
d. horizontal.

___21. If an Engel curve has a positive slope, then it can be concluded that the slope of the associated income-consumption curve is:
a. negative.
b. positive.
c. equal to zero.
d. equal to infinity.

___22. If a consumer is in the inelastic portion of the demand curve, then it can be concluded that the slope of the associated price-consumption curve is:
a. equal to zero.
b. equal to infinity.
c. positive.
d. negative.

___23. If the quantity of good Y (Q_Y) is on the vertical axis and Q_X is on the horizontal axis and the price of good Y decreases, then it can be concluded that the budget line will:
a. shift parallel to the original budget line.
b. rotate counter clockwise around the X axis.
c. rotate clockwise around the X axis.
d. rotate clockwise around the Y axis.

____24. If the price of good X (P$_X$) decreases in the process of finding the income and substitution effects, then the budget line must:
    a. rotate clockwise around the Y axis to a higher indifference curve.
    b. shift parallel toward the origin, back to original indifference curve, after first rotating.
    c. shift parallel out from the origin, back to original indifference curve, after first rotating.
    d. first have new X and Y intercepts resulting from the change in P$_X$.

____25. If good X is a Giffen good with a substitution effect of +9 units, then the:
    a. net effect is positive and less than 9 units.
    b. net effect is negative and more than 9 units.
    c. income effect is negative and less than 9 units.
    d. income effect is negative and more than 9 units.

Use Figure 4-1 to answer questions 26 -30. Assume the original equilibrium is point A on indifference curve U$_0$.

FIGURE 4-1

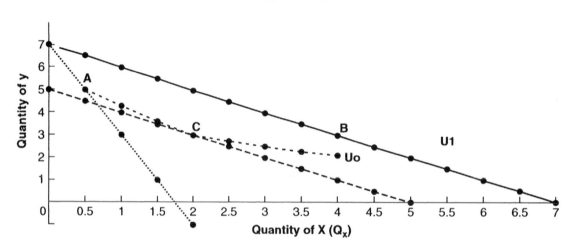

____26. What has happened to move from point A on U$_0$ to point B on U$_1$?
    a. Money income (I) has increased.
    b. The price of good Y (P$_Y$) has decreased.
    c. The price of good X (P$_X$) has decreased.
    d. The price of good X (P$_X$) has increased.

____27. What has happened to move from point B on U$_1$ to point C on U$_0$?
    a. Money income (I) has decreased.
    b. Money income (I) has increased.
    c. Both P$_X$ and P$_Y$ have increased.
    d. Both P$_X$ and P$_Y$ have decreased.

___28. The difference between point A and point C measures the:
    a. income effect.
    b. substitution effect.
    c. Veblen effect.
    d. marginal rate of substitution.

___29. The difference between point C and point B measures the:
    a. marginal rate of substitution.
    b. marginal utility of X.
    c. substitution effect.
    d. income effect.

___30. If the original equilibrium were at point B, then the substitution effect would be:
    a. measured between two points on U_1.
    b. along the budget line with X and Y intercepts of 5.
    c. along the budget line with X and Y intercepts of 7.
    d. measured between two points on U_0.

CHAPTER 5:

MARKET DEMAND AND ELASTICITIES

PART I: REVIEW OF CONCEPTS FROM PREVIOUS CHAPTER

Prior to reading chapter 5, match statements at left with the appropriate concept at right.

____1. Satisfaction from consuming a good   a. utility
____2. Change in consumption not caused by a price change   b. substitute goods
____3. Goods that satisfy the same consumer desires   c. law of demand
____4. Inverse relationship between price and quantity demanded   d. market
____5. A good that is in greater demand as consumer incomes rise   e. change in P
____6. A good for which demand falls as consumer incomes rise   f. inferior good
____7. Transactions between buyers and sellers occur here   g. shift in demand
____8. Causes a change in quantity demanded   h. normal good

PART II: ANNOTATED CHAPTER OUTLINE

5.1 THE MARKET DEMAND FOR A COMMODITY
1. **Market demand curve**: horizontal summation of the demand curves of all the consumers in the market
2. **Bandwagon effect**: people demand a commodity because others are purchasing it, to "keep up with the Joneses" or because it makes the commodity more useful
3. **Snob effect**: consumers seek to be different and exclusive by demanding less of a commodity as more people consume it
4. **Veblen effect**: consumers demanding more of certain commodities the more expensive these goods are ("conspicuous consumption")

5.2 PRICE ELASTICITY OF MARKET DEMAND
A. Measuring the Price Elasticity of Demand
1. The price elasticity of demand measures the responsiveness in the quantity demanded of a commodity to a change in its price
2. It is measured by calculating the value of ?, the coefficient of the price elasticity of demand, which is equal to the percentage change in the quantity demanded of the commodity divided by the percentage change in price
3. **Point elasticity of demand** is the measurement of the elasticity at a particular point on the demand curve.

4. **Arc elasticity of demand** is the measurement of the elasticity between two points on a demand curve.
5. Demand is said to be elastic if the absolute value of ? is greater than 1, inelastic if it is less than 1, and unitary elastic if it is equal to 1.

B. **Price Elasticity Graphically**
1. To measure the price elasticity at any point on a linear demand curve, drop a perpendicular from that point to the horizontal axis.
2. The distance along the horizontal axis from the original to the horizontal axis intercept of the demand curve is now cut into two segments; one from the original to the perpendicular (call this the left-hand piece) and one from the perpendicular to the horizontal intercept of the demand curve (call this the right-hand piece).
3. The value of the elasticity can then be calculated by taking the length of the right-hand piece and dividing it by the length of the left-hand piece.
4. Notice that while the slope of a straight-line demand curve is constant throughout, the price elasticity changes at each point. It is elastic above the midpoint, unitary at the midpoint, and inelastic below the midpoint.
5. If the demand curve is nonlinear, draw a straight-line tangent to the demand curve at the point where the elasticity is to be measured and proceed as above.

C. **Price Elasticity and Total Expenditures**
1. Total expenditures and price move in opposite directions if demand is elastic and in the same direction if demand is inelastic; total expenditures are constant as price changes when demand is unitary elastic.
2. A demand curve with price elasticity that is unitary throughout is a rectangular hyperbola.

D. **What Determines Price Elasticity?**
1. The price elasticity of demand for a commodity is larger the closer and greater are the number of available substitutes.
2. The price elasticity of demand for a commodity is larger the longer the period of time allowed for consumers to adjust to a change in the commodity price.

5.3 INCOME ELASTICITY OF DEMAND
1. **Engel curve**: showing the amount of a commodity that a consumer would purchase per unit of time at various income levels, while holding prices and tastes constant
2. **Income elasticity of demand**: measurement of responsiveness or sensitivity in the quantity demanded of a commodity at any point on the Engel curve.
3. To measure the income elasticity demand, calculate the value of the coefficient ?$_I$, which is equal to the percentage change in the quantity purchased divided by the percentage change in income.
4. **Necessity**: normal good with ?$_I$ between 0 and 1.
5. **Luxury**: normal good with ?$_I$ greater than 1.
6. **Engel's law**: the proportion of total expenditures on food declines as family incomes rise.

5.4 CROSS ELASTICITY OF DEMAND

1. **Substitutes**: if more of X is purchased when the price of Y goes up
2. **Complements**: if less of X is purchased when the price of Y goes up
3. **Cross elasticity of demand**: measurement of responsiveness or sensitivity in the quantity purchased of commodity X as a result of a change in the price of commodity Y
4. To measure the cross elasticity of demand, calculate the value of ? $_{XY}$ which is equal to the percentage change in the quantity of X demanded divided by the percentage change in the price of Y.
   a. if ? $_{XY}$ is greater than zero X and Y are substitutes.
   b. if ? $_{XY}$ is less than zero X and Y are complements.
   c. if ? $_{XY}$ is close to zero the two goods are independent commodities.

5.5 PRICE AND INCOME ELASTICITIES OF IMPORTS AND EXPORTS

1. **Price elasticity of demand for imports**: measurement of change in the quantity of U.S. imports resulting from a price change
2. **Price elasticity of demand for exports**: measurement of change in the quantity of U.S. exports resulting from a price change
3. **Exchange rate**: rate of exchange between the dollar and a foreign currency
4. **Income elasticity of demand for imports**: measurement of change in the quantity of U.S. imports resulting from an income or GDP change in the United States
5. **Income elasticity of demand for exports**: measurement of change in the quantity of U.S. exports resulting from an income or GDP change in other countries

5.6 MARGINAL REVENUE AND ELASTICITY

A. **Demand, Total Revenue, and Marginal Revenue**
   1. **Total revenue (TR)**: price times the quantity sold
   2. **Marginal revenue (MR)**: change in total revenue per unit change in the quantity sold
   3. **Average revenue (AR)**: TR divided by quantity, which is equal to price
B. **The Geometry of Marginal Revenue Determination**: for a straight-line demand curve, MR is located one-half the distance from the demand curve and the vertical axis. For a nonlinear demand curve, draw a tangent line and proceed as above.
B. **Marginal Revenue, Price and Elasticity**: $MR = P(1 + 1/?)$ (remember that the coefficient of the price elasticity of demand has a negative sign; if you use its absolute value, replace the plus sign in the formula with a minus sign)

⌘ AT THE FRONTIER ⌘
THE MARKETING REVOLUTION WITH MICROMARKETING

Marketing research approaches to demand estimation are being revolutionized and are becoming increasingly important as a result of new technological developments that permit micromarketing (detailed point-of-sale information).

PART III: KEY CONCEPTS IN THIS CHAPTER

1. The price elasticity of demand indicates how responsive **consumers/firms** are to changes in price.

2. If the percentage change in quantity demanded is greater than the percentage change in price, then demand is **elastic/inelastic**. If the percentage change in quantity demanded is smaller than the percentage change in price, then demand is **elastic/inelastic**.

3. If demand is elastic, then a 15% price reduction will cause quantity demanded to **rise/fall** by **more than/less than/exactly** 15%.

4. If demand is inelastic, then a 15% price increase will cause quantity demanded to **rise/fall** by **more than/less than/exactly** 15%.

5. If a 10% price increase results in a 10% decrease in quantity demanded, then the elasticity coefficient equals _____, so demand is _____.

6. If a 12% decrease in price causes quantity demanded to change in the opposite direction by 10% then the elasticity coefficient is **greater than/less than/equal to** one. In this case total expenditures by the consumer should **increase/decrease/stay the same**.

7. If the price of a good is increased and demand is elastic, quantity demanded will **rise/fall** by a **larger/smaller** percentage than the price change. Consequently, the seller's total revenue will **rise/fall**.

8. The most important determinants of demand elasticity are the number of _____ available and the _____ elapsed since a price change.

9. Ceteris paribus, the more substitutes a good has the **larger/smaller** the elasticity of demand for the good. The fewer the substitutes a good has the **larger/smaller** its elasticity of demand.

10. Other things being equal, the elasticity of demand for a good will be **greater/smaller** the longer the time that consumers have to adjust to a price change.

11. The elasticity of demand will generally be **larger/smaller** the greater the number of available substitutes.

12. A successful advertising campaign will make it appear that the advertised good has **many/few** substitutes. Hence the advertisement will **increase/decrease** the elasticity of demand for the advertised good.

13. If the price of sugar rises and the consumption of coffee decreases, the sugar and coffee are **substitutes/complements/unrelated goods**. Hence the cross elasticity coefficient is **positive/negative/zero** between the two goods.

14. If the price of tea decreases and the consumption of coffee decreases, then tea and coffee are **substitutes/complements/unrelated goods**. Hence the cross elasticity coefficient is **positive/negative/zero** between the two goods.

15. The income elasticity of Yakee Tingling Soda is −1.5. This signifies that a 5% increase in consumer's real income will cause consumers to consume _____ **more/less** Yakee Tingling Soda than previously. The negative coefficient means that Yakee Tingling Soda is a **normal/inferior** good.

16. The income elasticity of Hot Cake is 1.5. This signifies that a 6% increase in consumer's real income will cause consumers to consume _____ **more/less**

Hot Cake than previously. The positive coefficient means that Hot Cake is a **normal/inferior** good.

17. The _____ price elasticity between apples and oranges measures the responsiveness in quantity demanded for apples to a change in the price of oranges.

18. The cross price elasticity of demand between two goods is positive for _____ goods.

19. The _____ of demand measures the responsiveness in quantity demanded to a change in income.

20. If the income elasticity of demand for good X is negative, then the good is a(n) _____ good.

PART IV: MULTIPLE-CHOICE QUESTIONS

____1. The market demand curve is the:
   a. vertical summation of the demand curves of all consumers in the market.
   b. horizontal summation of the marginal revenue curves of all consumers in the market.
   c. difference between the values found on the demand curve and the marginal revenue curve at each quantity.
   d. horizontal summation of the demand curves of all consumers in the market.

____2. Using a geometric approach, the value of the coefficient of the price elasticity of demand (?) can be calculated by finding the:
   a. length of the section of the horizontal axis which starts at the perpendicular and extends to the horizontal intercept of the demand curve and dividing by the length of the section of the horizontal axis which starts at the origin and extends to the perpendicular.
   b. length of the section of the horizontal axis which starts at the origin and extends to the perpendicular and dividing by the length of the segment which starts at the perpendicular and extends to the horizontal intercept of the demand curve.
   c. lower section of the vertical axis which starts at the origin (to some positive price) divided into the remaining upper section.
   d. inverse of the slope of the demand curve (D).

____3. The income elasticity of demand is the:
   a. value set by the net income of the firm.
   b. percentage change in a consumer's income (I) divided by the percentage change in quantity (Q).
   c. percentage change in quantity (Q) divided by the percentage change in income (I).
   d. measured by moving from one point to another on the demand curve, ceteris paribus.

___4. The cross elasticity of demand is the:
   a. demand by one consumer x compared to the demand by another consumer y for the same good.
   b. percentage change in the quantity of good X divided by the percentage change in the price of good Y.
   c. percentage change in the price of good Y divided by the percentage change in the quantity of good X.
   d. measured by the substitution of input X for input Y in the production process.

___5. The form of the formula for calculating the price elasticity of demand for imports (or for exports) is:
   a. the same as the price elasticity of demand for goods consumed domestically.
   b. not the same as the price elasticity of demand for goods consumed domestically.
   c. not used since such elasticities do not exist.
   d. percentage change in the price of imports (exports) divided by the percentage change in quantity.

___6. If the price and the total revenue move in the opposite direction, then demand is:
   a. elastic.
   b. inelastic.
   c. unitary elastic.
   d. positively sloped.

___7. If the price (P) is equal to $10 and the marginal revenue (MR) is equal to $5, then the value of the coefficient of the price elasticity of demand is:
   a. -2.
   b. -1.
   c. 0.
   d. 0.5.

___8. If price (P) is equal to $10 and the price elasticity of demand is 2, then:
   a. total revenue (TR) is $20.
   b. marginal revenue (MR) at P = $10 is $5.
   c. average revenue (AR) is less than $10.
   d. average revenue (AR) is more than $10.

___9. If total revenue (TR) is declining, then:
   a. average revenue (AR) is negative and the AR curve has a negative slope.
   b. marginal revenue (MR) is negative and the MR curve has a negative slope.
   c. MR is zero and above AR.
   d. the slope of the TR curve is constant and MR is negative.

___10. Price (P) and average revenue (AR) are:
   a. always greater than the marginal revenue (MR).
   b. multiplied together to give total revenue (TR).
   c. always the same regardless of the market structure assumed.
   d. never the same regardless of the market structure assumed.

___11. The rate of exchange between the dollar and a foreign currency is:
   a. fixed by law.
   b. allowed to float for a month at a time.
   c. the price of the dollar in terms of the other currency.
   d. determined by the gold standard.

___12. If the cross elasticity of demand is equal to 4, and the change in the quantity demanded of good X is 8, then the change in the price of good Y is:
   a. $4 for these substitute goods.
   b. $1 for these complement goods.
   c. $2 for these substitute goods.
   d. infinity for these complement goods.

___13. The longer the time allowed for consumers to adjust to a change in the commodity price, the:
   a. more elastic is demand.
   b. more inelastic is demand.
   c. less elastic is demand.
   d. more likely that the absolute value of the price elasticity of demand (?) is less than 1.

___14. When the price elasticity of demand (?) is constant, the:
   a. slope of demand is constant.
   b. demand curve is a rectangular hyperbola.
   c. cross elasticity of demand is constant.
   d. income elasticity of demand is constant.

___15. A market demand curve is the:
   a. vertical summation of individual demand curves.
   b. sum of the marginal revenue (MR) curves.
   c. vertical summation of individual average revenue (AR) curves.
   d. horizontal summation of individual demand curves.

___16. The "snob effect" is"
   a. "keeping up with the Joneses."
   b. "conspicuous consumption."
   c. some individuals who consume less of a good because it is popular.
   d. a combination of the bandwagon effect and the Veblen effect.

____17. If a demand curve is not linear, then to calculate the value of the coefficient of the price elasticity of demand:
    a. simply pick two or more points on the curve and apply to these points the same geometric rules used on linear demand curves to calculate price elasticity of demand (?).
    b. draw a straight line tangent to the curve and then apply to this line the same geometric rules used on linear demand curves to calculate the price elasticity of demand (?).
    c. the price elasticity of demand (?) is constant.
    d. geometric rules cannot be used to calculate the value of (?).

____18. Given a demand curve with the equation $Q = \$100/P$, which of the following is true?
    a. The demand curve is a rectangular hyperbola and total expenditures are constant at $100.
    b. The demand curve is linear and total expenditures are not constant.
    c. Total expenditures are Q divided by P.
    d. Price elasticity of demand (?) is different at every point on the demand curve.

____19. The closer and greater the number of substitutes for a good:
    a. the less elastic is the demand for the good.
    b. the more elastic is the demand for the good.
    c. the more likely that ? will have a value equal to 1.
    d. the more likely that ? will have a value less than 1.

____20. Given that the %? Q of good X is less than the %? I (income), it can be concluded that good x is:
    a. an inferior good.
    b. a luxury good.
    c. a Giffen good.
    d. a normal good.

____21. The proportion of total expenditures on food declines as family income rises according to:
    a. the law of demand.
    b. the snob effect.
    c. the bandwagon effect.
    d. Engel's law.

____22. The income elasticity of demand ($?_I$) for imports in the United States:
    a. is less than 1 indicating that imports are inferior goods.
    b. is greater than 1 indicating that imports increase less than the percentage increase in U.S. income.
    c. is estimated to be 1.94% indicating that imports increase 19.4% for each 10% increase in U.S. income.
    d. is less than the short-run price elasticity of demand for U.S. manufactured goods exported.

_____23. MR is equal to:
   a. $P(1 - 1/?)$.
   b. $P(1 + ?)$.
   c. $P(1 - ?)$.
   d. $P(1 + 1/?)$.

For questions 24 - 28 the demand curve is given by the equation Q = 24 - 8P.

_____24. If the equilibrium price (P) is $1.50, then the price elasticity of demand (?) is:
   a. unitary.
   b. 1.5.
   c. inelastic.
   d. Cannot be determined from the information provided.

_____25. If P increases from $1.50 to $2.00, then:
   a. the demand is more inelastic.
   b. the demand is less elastic.
   c. ? increases to 2.
   d. ? decreases to 0.5.

_____26. If P decreases from $1.50 to $1.00, then:
   a. ? increases to 2.
   b. ? decreases to 0.5.
   c. the demand is less inelastic.
   d. the demand is more elastic.

_____27. When P = $1.50 then P(24 - 8P) represents:
   a. marginal revenue (MR) = $1.50.
   b. average revenue (AR) = $12.00.
   c. the price elasticity of demand (?).
   d. total expenditures = $18.

_____28. If this demand curve shifts to the left with a vertical axis intercept of $2.00 and a horizontal axis intercept of 16, then at price (P) of good X = $1.50, the price elasticity of demand (?) is:
   a. more inelastic than before the shift.
   b. equal to 0.25.
   c. equal to 4, more elastic than before the shift.
   d. not possible to calculate with the information provided.

_____29. Price rises from $12 to $14 and the quantity demanded falls from 80 units to 60 units. What is the price elasticity of demand between the two points?
   a. approximately 1.86.
   b. approximately 0.8.
   c. approximately 0.5.
   d. 1.

___30. If the price of good X falls and the demand for X is elastic, then:

    a.   the percentage rise in quantity demanded is greater than the percentage fall in price and total revenue rises.

    b.   the percentage rise in quantity demanded is less than the percentage fall in price and total revenue falls.

    c.   the percentage rise in quantity demanded is greater than the percentage fall in price and total revenue falls.

    d.   the percentage fall in quantity demanded is greater than the percentage fall in price and total revenue falls.

CHAPTER 6:

CHOICE
UNDER UNCERTAINTY

PART I: REVIEW OF CONCEPTS FROM PREVIOUS CHAPTER

Prior to reading chapter 6, match statements at left with the appropriate concept at right.

____1. Measures the responsiveness of quantity supplied to price changes
____2. These two goods have a negative cross price elasticity
____3. People consume less of it as their income increases
____4. When the price of X decreases people consume less of Y
____5. When the price of X decreases people consume the same amount of Y
____6. If the price falls and total revenues rise, demand is _____
____7. This inferior good has a positively sloped demand curve
____8. Shows the amount of a good that the consumer would purchase per unit of time at various income levels
____9. Locus of consumer optimum points resulting when only consumer's income varies
____10. Everything else held constant
____11. People consume less of it as their income declines
____12. Method used to show the indifference curves for two individuals each consuming the same two goods and the path to equilibrium through mutually beneficial exchange

a. normal good
b. substitutes
c. supply elasticity
d. inferior good
e. complements
f. unrelated goods
g. ceteris paribus
h. elastic
i. Giffen good
j. Edgeworth box
k. income-consumption curve
l. Engel curve

PART II: ANNOTATED CHAPTER OUTLINE

6.1 RISK AND UNCERTAINTY IN DEMAND CHOICES
1. **Certainty**: the situation when there is only one possible outcome to a decision and this outcome is known precisely
2. **Risk**: the situation where there is more than one possible outcome to a decision and the probability of each specific outcome is known or can be estimated
3. **Uncertainty**: the case when there is more than one possible outcome to a decision and where the probability of each specific outcome occurring is not known or even meaningful

4. Choices involving risk or uncertainty are analyzed using the concepts of:
    a. **strategy**: one of several alternative courses of action that a decision maker can undertake to achieve a goal
    b. **states of nature**: conditions in the future that will have a significant effect on the degree of success or failure of any strategy
    c. **payoff matrix**: a table that shows the possible outcomes or results of each strategy under each state of nature

6.2 MEASURING RISK
A. Probability Distributions
1. **Probability**: the chance or odds that the event will occur
2. **Probability distribution**: a list of all the possible outcomes of an event and the probability attached to each
B. The Standard Deviation: measures the dispersion of possible outcomes from the expected value

6.3 UTILITY THEORY AND RISK AVERSION
A. Different Preferences Toward Risk
1. **Risk averters**: individuals who seek to minimize risks
2. **Risk seekers or risk lovers**: may choose the more risky investment
3. **Risk neutral** individuals are indifferent to risk
4. **Diminishing marginal utility of money**: each additional unit of money has less extra utility. Explains why most individuals are risk averters: a person would gain less utility by winning some amount of money than the utility he or she would lose in losing the same amount of money.
B. Maximize Expected Utility
1. Even if the expected monetary gain is positive a risk-averse manager will not make the investment if the expected utility of the investment is negative
2. The general rule is that the individual seeks to maximize utility in a world of no risk or uncertainty, but maximizes expected utility in the face of risk

6.4 INSURANCE AND GAMBLING
A. Why Do Some Individuals Buy Insurance?
1. A risk averter will be willing to pay a small amount of money to avoid the risk of incurring a large loss
2. **Risk premium**: the maximum amount that the individual would be willing to pay to avoid the risk
B. Why Do Some Individuals Gamble?
1. An individual is willing to pay a small sum to have a chance at winning a large sum.

6.5 RISK AVERSION AND INDIFFERENCE CURVES
1. Indifference curves can be drawn showing all the combination of standard deviation and expected income that give the individual the same level of utility or satisfaction.
2. The more risk-averse the individual, the greater the increase in expected income that will be needed to compensate for an increase in the standard deviation and still leave the individual on the same indifference curve.

6.6 REDUCING RISK AND UNCERTAINTY
A. Gathering More Information
1. Individuals and decision-makers can often make better predictions and sharply reduce the risk or uncertainty surrounding a particular strategy or event by collecting more information.
2. However, gathering information is costly, and so the individual should only continue to gather information until the marginal cost equals the marginal benefit.

B. Diversification
1. Diversification means spreading the risks.
2. If there is perfect negative correlation between two activities the risk can be entirely eliminated by engaging in both activities at the same time.

C. Insurance
1. Risk averters can avoid risk by purchasing insurance.

⌘ **AT THE FRONTIER** ⌘
FOREIGN EXCHANGE RISKS AND HEDGING

Investing in foreign securities gives rise to a foreign-exchange risk because the foreign currency can depreciate or decrease in value during the time of the investment. Hedging refers to the covering of a foreign-exchange risk; it is usually accomplished with a forward contract or a futures contract. Hedging reduces transactions costs and risks and increases the volume of domestic and foreign trade in the commodity, currency, or other financial instrument.

PART III: KEY CONCEPTS IN THIS CHAPTER

1. If there is only one possible outcome to a decision and it is known precisely it is a situation of _____.

2. If there is more than one possible outcome to a decision and the probability of each specific outcome is known or can be estimated it is a situation of _____.

3. If there is more than one possible outcome to a decision and the probability of each specific outcome is unknown or not meaningful it is a situation of _____.

4. Suppose you enter a game involving the toss of a fair coin. If the coin turns up heads you win $10; if it turns up tails you win nothing. Is this a situation of risk or uncertainty?

5. One of several alternative courses of action that a decision-maker can take to achieve a goal is a _____.

6. The dispersion of possible outcomes from the expected value is measured by the _____.

7. Individuals who seek to minimize risks are called **risk averters/lovers/neutral**.

8. Most individuals are risk **averters/lovers/neutral** because they face **diminishing/increasing** marginal utility of money.
9. In the face of risk, individuals seek to maximize **utility/expected monetary return/expected utility**.
10. A person who buys insurance is likely to be a risk **averter/lover**.
11. The same individual could purchase insurance and also gamble. True or false?
12. Indifference curves showing the tradeoff between expected income and standard deviation are **positively/negatively** sloped.
13. The more risk-averse the individual, the **steeper/flatter** the indifference curves showing the tradeoff between expected income and standard deviation for that individual.
14. An individual can reduce risk by **gambling/purchasing insurance**.
15. Spreading the risk is called _____
16. Risk can be eliminated by engaging in activities that have perfect **negative/positive** correlation.
17. The maximum price that an individual is willing to pay for insurance is equal to the _____ premium.
18. Insurance that is fairly priced or actuarially fair is **greater than/equal to/less than** the expected loss that it covers.
19. Hedging can be accomplished with either a _____ contract or a _____ contract.
20. Futures markets exist not only in currencies but also in many other financial instruments or derivatives and commodities. True or false?

PART IV: MULTIPLE-CHOICE QUESTIONS

____1. Investing in Treasury bills is an example of a situation of:
   a. certainty.
   b. risk.
   c. uncertainty.
   d. hedging.

____2. Investing in a stock and tossing a coin are both situations of:
   a. certainty.
   b. risk.
   c. uncertainty.
   d. None of the above; tossing a coin involves risk but buying stock is a situation of uncertainty.

____3. Drilling for oil is a situation of:
   a. certainty.
   b. risk.
   c. uncertainty
   d. hedging.

_____4. Conditions in the future that will have a significant effect on the results of a decision are referred to as:
   a. strategies.
   b. a payoff matrix.
   c. states of nature.
   d. risks.

_____5. When considering a payoff matrix, it is up to the individual to choose:
   a. the strategies.
   b. the states of nature.
   c. both the strategies and the states of nature.
   d. neither the strategies nor the states of nature.

_____6. Lower risk is associated with a _____ standard deviation.
   a. positive
   b. negative
   c. larger
   d. smaller

_____7. The dispersion of possible outcomes from the expected value is measured by the:
   a. probability.
   b. probability difference.
   c. standard deviation.
   d. horizontal axis.

_____8. Most individuals are:
   a. risk averters.
   b. risk lovers.
   c. risk neutral.
   d. hedgers.

_____9. Individuals who choose a more risky investment are:
   a. risk averters.
   b. risk lovers.
   c. risk neutral.
   d. hedgers.

_____10. An individual who is indifferent to risk would be described as:
   a. a risk averter.
   b. a risk lover.
   c. risk neutral.
   d. a hedger.

_____11. Most individuals who are risk averters are so because they face:
   a. diminishing marginal utility of money.
   b. increasing marginal utility of money.
   c. diminishing total utility of money.
   d. increasing total utility of money.

____12. As a result of diminishing marginal utility of money, the total utility curve is:
    a. horizontal.
    b. vertical.
    c. concave.
    d. convex.

____13. Individuals are risk averters when:
    a. the gain in utility from winning a particular sum of money is less than the loss in utility from losing the same sum.
    b. the gain in utility from winning a particular sum of money is greater than the loss in utility from losing the same sum.
    c. the gain in utility from winning a particular sum of money is the same as the loss in utility from losing the same sum.
    d. they prefer to gamble than buy insurance.

____14. Suppose a person is engaged in a bet to win $100 if "heads" turns up in the tossing of a coin or lose $100 if "tails" comes up. Assume that the coin is fair. The expected value of the return from this bet is:
    a. $100.
    b. $200.
    c. -$100.
    d. 0.

____15. Suppose a person is engaged in a bet to win $100 if "heads" turns up in the tossing of a coin or lose $100 if "tails" comes up. The person would lose 2 utils by losing $100, and gain 1 util by winning $100. Assume that the coin is fair. The expected utility of this bet is:
    a. 0.
    b. 0.5.
    c. -0.5.
    d. $100.

____16. Even if the expected monetary return of an investment is positive, a _____ manager will not make the investment if the expected utility of the investment is negative.
    a. risk-loving
    b. risk-averse
    c. risk-neutral
    d. All of the above.

____17. One reason for America's craze for gambling may be that many individuals may be _____ for small gambles but _____ for big gambles.
    a. risk averters; risk lovers
    b. risk lovers; risk averters
    c. risk averters; risk neutral
    d. risk neutral; risk lovers

___18. An individual who buys insurance prefers a given sum of money with certainty to a risky asset of _____ expected value.
   a. greater
   b. smaller
   c. equal
   d. unknown

___19. The maximum amount that the individual would be willing to pay to avoid a risk is called the:
   a. expected value.
   b. utility price.
   c. risk premium.
   d. hedge price.

___20. An individual who both purchases insurance and gambles would have a total utility of money curve that is:
   a. concave.
   b. convex.
   c. concave at low levels of money income and convex at higher levels of income.
   d. convex at low levels of money income and concave at higher levels of income.

___21. Indifference curves that relate expected income to standard deviation are:
   a. upward sloping.
   b. downward sloping.
   c. vertical.
   d. horizontal.

___22. The more risk averse the individual, the _____ the indifference curve relating expected income to standard deviation.
   a. flatter
   b. steeper
   c. more concave
   d. more convex

___23. Suppose that individual A requires an additional $40 in expected income to compensate him or her for an increase in the standard deviation from 0.5 to 1.0, while individual B requires an additional $20 to compensate for the same increase in the standard deviation. We can conclude that:
   a. individual A is more risk averse.
   b. individual B is less risk averse.
   c. individual A is risk neutral.
   d. individual B is risk neutral.

___24. An individual can reduce risk or uncertainty by:
   a. gathering more information.
   b. diversification.
   c. purchasing insurance.
   d. All of the above.

____25. Consulting *Consumer Reports* for information about brands of appliances is an example of reducing risk through:
   a. gathering more information.
   b. diversification.
   c. purchasing insurance.
   d. hedging.

____26. "Don't put all of your eggs in one basket" refers to the idea that you can reduce risk by:
   a. gathering more information.
   b. diversification.
   c. purchasing insurance.
   d. All of the above.

____27. If there is perfect negative correlation between two activities then risk can be eliminated by engaging in both activities at the same time. This is an example of reducing risk through:
   a. gathering more information.
   b. diversification.
   c. purchasing insurance.
   d. All of the above.

____28. Insurance whose price is equal to the expected loss that it covers is referred to as:
   a. fairly priced.
   b. actuarially fair.
   c. zero insurance premium.
   d. Both a and b.

____29. Suppose that you invest $10,000 in a European security that promises to pay a 10% return when the exchange rate is $1 to one euro. If the euro depreciates by 5%, your net dollar return will be:
   a. 10%.
   b. 15%.
   c. 5%.
   d. 0.

____30. Foreign exchange risk can be covered with a:
   a. forward contract.
   b. futures contract.
   c. exchange rate.
   d. Both a and b.

CHAPTER 7:

PRODUCTION THEORY

Prior to reading chapter 7, match statements at left with the appropriate concept at right.

___1. Situation where there is more than one possible outcome
      and the probability of each outcome is known
___2. Measure of the dispersion of possible outcomes from
      the expected value
___3. Name for individuals who seek to minimize risks
___4. What individuals seek to maximize in the face of risk
___5. Spreading the risk
___6. The maximum price an individual would pay to avoid risk
___7. Covering foreign exchange risk
___8. The chance or odds that an event will occur
___9. For most individuals the marginal utility of money
___10. Name for individuals who seek to maximize risks

a. risk lovers
b. risk premium
c. risk
d. hedging
e. probability
f. diversification
g. diminishes
h. risk averse
i. expected utility
j. standard deviation

PART II: ANNOTATED CHAPTER OUTLINE

7.1 RELATING OUTPUTS TO INPUTS
  A. Organization of Production
  1. **Production**: transformation of resources or inputs into outputs of goods and services
  2. **Firm**: organization that combines and organizes resources to produce goods and services for sale at a profit
  B. Classification of Inputs
  1. **Inputs**: resources or factors of production used to produce goods and services; classified broadly into labor or human resources (including entrepreneurial talent), capital or investment goods, and land or natural resources
  2. **Entrepreneurship**: the ability of some individuals to see opportunities to combine resources in new and more efficient ways to produce a particular commodity or to produce entirely new commodities
  3. **Fixed inputs**: resources which cannot be varied (or can be varied only with excessive cost) during the time period under consideration
  4. **Variable inputs**: resources which can be varied easily and on short notice during the time period under consideration
  5. **Short run**: time period during which at least one input is fixed

6. **Long run**: time period during which all inputs can be varied

7.2 PRODUCTION WITH ONE VARIABLE INPUT
A. Total, Average, and Marginal Product
1. **Production function**: a unique relationship between inputs and outputs
2. **Total Product (TP)**: the output per period of time
3. **Average product of labor (AP_L)**: TP divided by the quantity of L used
4. **Marginal product of labor (MP_L)**: the change in TP divided by the change in L used
B. The Geometry of Average and Marginal Product Curves
1. AP_L at any point on the TP curve is equal to the slope of a straight line drawn from the origin to that point on the TP curve
2. MP_L between any two points on the TP curve is equal to the slope of the TP curve between those two points
C. The Law of Diminishing Returns: as more units of a variable input are used with a fixed amount of other inputs, after a point, a smaller and smaller return will accrue to each additional unit of the variable input (the MP of the variable input eventually declines)

7.3 PRODUCTION WITH TWO VARIABLE INPUTS
A. What Do Isoquants Show?
1. Isoquants show various combinations of two inputs that can be used to produce a specific level of output.
2. A higher isoquant (further from the origin) refers to a larger output, whereas a lower isoquant refers to a smaller output.
B. Derivation of Total Product Curves from the Isoquant Map
1. If we draw a horizontal line across an isoquant map at the level at which the input measured along the vertical axis is fixed then we can generate the total product curve for the variable input measured along the horizontal axis.
2. We can find the output level from the isoquant and then find the amount of the variable input (read off the horizontal axis) which, when combined with the fixed input, results in that amount of output

7.4 THE SHAPE OF ISOQUANTS
A. Characteristics of Isoquants
1. Negatively sloped in economically relevant range
2. Convex to the origin (looking away from the origin)
3. Do not intersect
4. Slope equals the marginal rate of technical substitution (MRTS, usually written as $MRTS_{LK}$ meaning substitution of L for K, meaning of labor for capital): the change in K divided by the change in L (assuming L is on the horizontal axis). Equals the ratio of the marginal products of the two inputs.
B. Economic Region of Production (assuming L is on the horizontal axis)
1. **Ridge lines**: separate the relevant (i.e., negatively sloped) portions of the isoquants from the irrelevant (i.e., positively sloped) portions
2. **Bottom ridge lines**: $MP_L = MRTS_{LK} = 0$
3. **Top ridge lines**: $MP_K = 0$ and $MRTS_{LK} = $ infinity

C. **Fixed-Proportions Production Functions**: isoquants shaped as the letter L (with origin of each having a fixed K/L ratio)

7.5 CONSTANT, INCREASING, AND DECREASING RETURNS TO SCALE
A. **Constant Returns to Scale**
   1. when output changes by the same proportion as inputs
B. **Increasing Returns to Scale**
   1. when output changes by a greater proportion than inputs
   2. arise because as the scale of operation increase, a greater division of labor and specialization can take place and more specialized and productive machinery can be used
C. **Decreasing Returns to Scale**
   1. when output changes by a smaller proportion than inputs
   2. arise because as the scale of operation increases it becomes ever more difficult to manage the firm effectively and coordinate the various operations and divisions of the firm

7.6 TECHNOLOGICAL PROGRESS AND INTERNATIONAL COMPETITIVENESS
A. **Meaning and Importance of Innovations**
   1. **Technological progress**: the development of new and better production techniques
   2. **Product innovation**: the introduction of new or improved products
   3. **Process innovation**: the introduction of new or improved processes
B. **Innovations and the International Competitiveness of U.S. Firms**
   1. **Product cycle model**: firms with innovations lose export markets and domestic markets to foreign imitators
   2. **Intraindustry trade**: the basis for much of international trade among industrial nations; trade in differentiated manufactured products

---

⌘   AT THE FRONTIER   ⌘
THE NEW COMPUTER-AIDED PRODUCTION REVOLUTION AND THE INTERNATIONAL COMPETITIVENESS OF U.S. FIRMS

Computer-aided design (CAD): allows research and development engineers to design a new product or component on a computer screen, quickly experiment with different alternative designs, and test their strength and reliability. Computer-aided manufacturing: issues instructions to a network of integrated machine tools to produce a prototype of the new or changed product.

PART III: KEY CONCEPTS IN THIS CHAPTER

1.   The inputs that do not vary as production is raised are called _____.

2. The _____ is the relationship between the maximum output that can be produced per period of time and inputs such as land, labor, capital, and entrepreneurship.
3. The _____ is the change in total product divided by the change in inputs.
4. The law of _____ states that after a point, the marginal product of the variable input declines due to the existence of fixed inputs.
5. _____ show the various combinations of two inputs that can be used to produce a specific level of output.
6. An increase in the stock of capital will cause a(n) _____ shift in the total product curve.
7. The optimal production technique involving two or more inputs requires that the ratio of _____ be equal to the ratio of _____ for all inputs involved in the production process.
8. The isoquants are _____ sloped in the economically relevant range, are _____ to the origin, and do/do not intersect.
9. The change in capital divided by the change in labor, which equals the ratio of the marginal products of the two inputs is called the _____.
10. In the long run, the law of diminishing marginal returns **is/is not** applicable since there are no fixed inputs. Hence, the relevant question in the long run becomes that of _____ to _____.
11. When output increases by a larger proportion than inputs, the firm must be experiencing a(n) _____ to scale. This phenomenon is relevant to the **short run/long run**.
12. The development of new and better production techniques is _____. Whereas the introduction of new or improved processes is called _____.
13. The model that stipulates that firms lose export markets and domestic markets to foreign imitators is the _____ model.
14. If the firm increases all of its inputs by 25%, and output increases by 25%, the firm must is experiencing **increasing/decreasing/constant** returns to scale.
15. The slope of an isoquant is the negative ratio of the _____ of the two inputs.
16. Isoquants that are L-shaped indicate a _____ production function.
17. The further the isoquant is from the origin, the **greater/smaller** the level of output it represents.
18. A firm would not operate above a ridge line where the isoquants were **negatively/positively** sloped.
19. Increasing returns to scale can be illustrated by isoquants that become **closer together/further apart** as we move along a ray away from the origin.
20. A production function that is homogeneous of degree 1 means that there will be _____ returns to scale.

PART IV: MULTIPLE-CHOICE QUESTIONS

___1. Total product (TP), bales of cotton, associated with the first five units of the variable input labor (L) (assuming a fixed amount of land) are 5, 12, 19, 27, and 36. The marginal product (MP) of increasing from the third to the fourth unit of L is:
   a. 19 bales.

b. 36 bales.

c. 8 bales.

d. 6.33 bales.

___2. Marginal product (MP), bushels of corn, associated with the first five units of the variable input labor (L) (assuming a fixed amount of land) are 3, 5, 4, 3, and 1. The total product (TP) of the first three units of L is:

a. –12 bushels.

b. 12 bushels.

c. 4 bushels.

d. –4 bushels.

___3. Total product (TP), feet of rope, as associated with the three units of the variable input labor (L) (assuming a fixed amount of land) is 14. Marginal product (MP) associated with an increase from the third to fourth unit of L is 6. What is the average product of four units of L?

a. 5 feet.

b. 14 feet.

c. 6 feet.

d. 20 feet.

___4. If marginal product (MP) associated with increasing the variable input labor (L) (assuming a fixed amount of capital) from the first to the second unit is 5, and from the second to the third unit is 4:

a. the total product (TP) associated with the third unit is 9.

b. the slope of the total product (TP) curve is increasing at an increasing rate.

c. the average product (AP) of L is falling.

d. the average product (AP) of L may be increasing or decreasing.

___5. The marginal product of labor (MP_L) curve reaches its maximum point:

a. after the average product of labor (AP_L) curve.

b. at the same quantity of labor as the average product of labor (AP_L) curve.

c. before the average product of labor (AP_L) curve.

d. None of the above; the MP_L never reaches a maximum.

___6. The average product of labor (AP_L) curve and the marginal product of labor curve (MP_L) intersect where:

a. the AP_L is at its lowest point.

b. the AP_L is at its highest point.

c. the MP_L is at its lowest point.

d. the MP_L is at its highest point.

Assume a two-variable input production function utilizing labor (L), which is on the horizontal axis, and capital (K), which is on the vertical axis. Use the following table to answer questions 7 – 11:

K ? / L ?	1	2	3	4	5
1	3	5	9	10	10
2	5	7	10	14	17
3	8	10	14	20	25
4	8	10	14	22	24
5	4	6	14	23	24

___7. Showing at least three combinations of inputs, identify the isoquant that would result in the quantity of output, Q, equal to 14 units:
   a. L = 3, K = 2; L = 3, K = 3; L = 3, K = 4.
   b. L = 4, K = 2; L = 2, K = 3; L = 3, K = 4.
   c. L = 4, K = 2; L = 3, K = 3; L = 3, K = 4.
   d. L = 2, K = 4; L = 3, K = 3; L = 3, K = 4.

___8. Showing at least three combinations of inputs, identify the isoquant that would result in the quantity of output, Q, equal to 10 units:
   a. L = 4, K = 1; L = 3, K = 2; L = 3, K = 3.
   b. L = 3, K = 1; L = 3, K = 2; L = 3, K = 3.
   c. L = 4, K = 1; L = 3, K = 2; L = 4, K = 2.
   d. L = 4, K = 1; L = 2, K = 5; L = 3, K = 3.

___9. Use the isoquant identified in question 7 to calculate the absolute value of the marginal rate of technical substitution (MRTS) of L for K (exclude values at which MRTS of L for K equals infinity). The MRTS of L for K is:
   a. the change in L divided by the change in K and is equal to 14.
   b. L divided by K and is equal to 2/4 = 0.5.
   c. the change in K divided by the change in L and is equal to +1.0.
   d. K divided by L and is equal to 3/3 = 1.0.

___10. Along the isoquant that would result in the quantity of output, Q, = 10 identify the input combinations that would form one of the borders of the ridge lines.
   a. L = 3, K = 3, 4 and 5
   b. K = 1, L = 3 and 4
   c. K = 2 and 3, L = 2 and 3
   d. K = 1, L = 4 and 5

___11. Holding capital (K) constant, identify the short-run production function that results in the maximum possible quantity of output, Q.
   a. K = 3, L = 5
   b. K = 25, L = 25
   c. K = 3, L = 25
   d. K = 5, L = 5

____12. Assume that capital (K) and labor (L) are infinitesimally divisible. Given a two variable input production function utilizing L (on the horizontal axis) and K (on the vertical axis):

    a. the ridge lines define the economic region of production, and connect the points along various isoquants at which the $MRTS_{LK}$ is equal to zero for the lowest ridge line and the $MRTS_{LK}$ is equal to infinity for the highest ridge line.

    b. the ridge lines define the economic region of production, and connect the points along various isoquants at which the $MRTS_{LK}$ is equal to infinity for the lowest ridge line and the $MRTS_{LK}$ is equal to zero for the highest ridge line.

    c. the ridge lines define the economic region of production, and connect the points along various isoquants at which the $MRTS_{LK}$ is equal to zero for the highest ridge line and the $MRTS_{LK}$ is equal to infinity for the lowest ridge line.

    d. the rational range of production is below the lowest ridge line and above the highest ridge line.

____13. Assume a two-variable input production function utilizing labor (L), which is on the horizontal axis, and capital (K), which is one the vertical axis. Assume that K/L is a constant for each of the most efficient production possibilities. Which of the following is true?

    a. The MRTS of L for K is always equal to infinity.

    b. The MRTS of L for K is always equal to zero.

    c. The MRTS of L for K is never equal to infinity nor zero.

    d. The slope of the isoquant is made up of two parts, one part vertical and one part horizontal.

____14. A two variable input production function utilizes labor (L) and capital (K) with initial values $L_1 = 4$, $K_1 = 2$, and quantity of output $Q_1 = 50$. Final values are $L_2 = 6$, $K_2 = 3$, and $Q_2 = 75$. What returns to scale are present?

    a. Increasing returns to scale because Q is larger than either input.

    b. Decreasing returns to scale because fewer units of K are used compared to units of L.

    c. Constant returns to scale since Q increases by the same percentage as the percentage increase of each of the inputs.

    d. Increasing returns to scale when you increase both inputs and decreasing returns to scale when you decrease both inputs.

____15. The Hildred Company makes machine parts necessary for the rockets used in the space program. The production process is very capital (K) intensive. Hildred engineers have found that the following relationships hold as they try to expand the quantity of output, Q, to meet the needs of the space program: Labor, $L_1 = 100$, $K_1 = 10,000$ and $Q_1 = 10$; $L_2 = 200$, $K_2 = 20,000$ and $Q_2 = 15$. What returns to scale are present?

    a. Increasing returns to scale since all values increase.

    b. Decreasing returns to scale since both inputs increased 100% but the output increased only 50%.

    c. Constant returns to scale since each of the inputs increases by the same amount, 100%.

  d. Decreasing returns to scale when you increase both inputs and increasing returns to scale when you decrease both inputs.

___16. In the real world, most firms seem to exhibit near:
  a. increasing returns to scale.
  b. decreasing returns to scale.
  c. constant returns to scale.
  d. None of the above; returns to scale is a theoretical construct that has no counterpart in reality.

___17. Technological progress refers to:
  a. the introduction of new improved products.
  b. the introduction of new or improved production processes.
  c. the investment in human capital.
  d. the development of new and better production techniques.

___18. Most innovations are:
  a. found by U.S. firms.
  b. incremental and involve continuous small improvements.
  c. found in single, major technological breakthroughs.
  d. not measured by new isoquant maps.

___19. Strong domestic rivalry and geographic concentration stimulate:
  a. antitrust legislation in the United States.
  b. inventions in Japan.
  c. innovations in Japan.
  d. the product cycle.

___20. According to the _____ model, firms that first introduce an innovation eventually lose their export market and their domestic market to foreign imitators who pay lower wages and have generally lower costs.
  a. product cycle
  b. production possibilities
  c. supply and demand
  d. comparative advantage

___21. Firms can exploit the benefits of successful innovations:
  a. because they are adequately protected by international patent law.
  b. forever.
  c. for shorter and shorter periods before foreign imitators take away the market.
  d. because they are adequately protected by domestic patent law.

___22. The law of diminishing returns applies because:
  a. increasing returns to scale are exhausted.
  b. at least one input is more inefficient that the others.
  c. at least one input is paid more than the others.
  d. each additional unit of the variable input has less and less of the fixed inputs with which to work.

____23. An isoquant shows the various combinations of:
   a. a fixed input and a variable input that give the same level of output.
   b. two commodities that provide the consumer equal satisfaction.
   c. two inputs that give the same level of output.
   d. two commodities that provide the consumer equal satisfaction, assuming that their prices are the same.

____24. The marginal rate of technical substitution (MRTS) of labor (L) for capital (K) is:
   a. the slope of the total product (TP) curve.
   b. the marginal product of labor (MP_L) divided by the average product of labor (AP_L).
   c. analogous to the marginal rate of substitution (MRS) of one good for another in consumption, which MRS is given by the absolute value of the slope of the indifference curve.
   d. analogous to the MRS of one good for another in consumption, which MRS is given by the slope of the isoquant.

Assume that the variable input labor time (L) is infinitesimally divisible and that the amount of capital (K) is fixed. Use Figure 7-1 to answer questions 25 – 29:

FIGURE 7-1

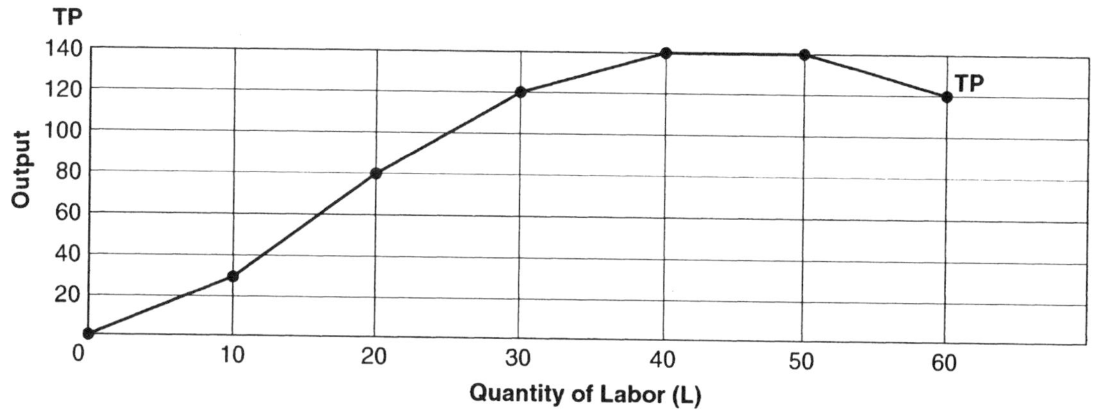

____25. At approximately what value for L is the average product of labor (AP_L) equal to the marginal product of labor (MP_L)?
   a. 45
   b. 20
   c. 15
   d. 25

____26. What is the value of the marginal product of labor (MP_L) at $L = 45$?
   a. zero
   b. $140/40 = 3.5$
   c. $140/50 = 2.8$
   d. $[140/40 + 140/50]/2 = 3.15$

____27. Note that the total product of labor (TP_L) is 120 when the quantity of labor (L) is 30 and 60. What can be concluded?
   a. The AP_L at the two points are equal.
   b. The AP_L have equal but opposite signs at the two points.
   c. The MP_L between $L = 30$ and $L = 40$ is equal to the MP_L between points $L = 50$ and $L = 60$.
   d. The MP_L between points $L = 30$ and $L = 40$ is less than the MP_L between points $L = 50$ and $L = 60$.

____28. A ray from the origin to the point on the TP curve where $Q = 120$ and $L = 60$ measures:
   a. the slope at that point which is a MP_L of -2.
   b. the inflection point where AP_L equals MP_L at a value of 4.
   c. the $AP_L = 120/60 = 2$.
   d. the $AP_L = 120/2 = 60$.

____29. In the economic region of production:
   a. the MP_L is positive and declining and the MP_K is negative.
   b. the MP_K is positive and declining and the MP_L is negative.
   c. the MP_L and the MP_K are both negative but rising.
   d. the MP_L and the MP_K are both positive but declining.

____ 30. Homogeneous of degree 1 means:
   a. increasing returns to scale.
   b. decreasing returns to scale.
   c. constant returns to scale.
   d. no implications for returns to scale.

CHAPTER 8:

COSTS OF PRODUCTION

PART I: REVIEW OF CONCEPTS FROM PREVIOUS CHAPTER

Prior to reading chapter 8, match statements at left with the appropriate concept at right.

___1. Combining resources to create goods and services

___2. Organization that transforms inputs into outputs

___3. Land, labor, capital and entrepreneurship

___4. Additional or incremental units

___5. Human factor of production

___6. Non-human factor of production

___7. Highest benefits forfeited when taking an action

___8. Knowledge about how to use resources to produce goods

___9. Time period during which some inputs are fixed

___10. Shows various combinations of two inputs that can be used to produce a specific level of output

___11. Time period during which all inputs are variable

___12. Introduction of new or improved products

___13. When output changes by a smaller proportion than the change in inputs

a. inputs
b. firm
c. capital
d. marginal product
e. technology
f. opportunity cost
g. production
h. labor
i. short run
j. long run
k. decreasing returns
l. product innovation
m. isoquants

PART II: ANNOTATED CHAPTER OUTLINE

8.1 THE NATURE OF PRODUCTION COSTS

1. **Explicit costs**: actual out-of-pocket expenditures of the firm to purchase or hire the inputs it requires in production

2. **Implicit costs**: value of the inputs owned and used by the firm in its own production processes

3. **Alternative or opportunity cost doctrine**: for a firm to retain any input for its own use, it must include as a cost what the input could earn in its best alternative use or employment

4. **Private costs**: opportunity costs incurred by individuals and firms in the process of producing goods and services

5. **Social costs**: costs incurred by society as a whole

8.2 COST IN THE SHORT RUN

A. Total Costs

1. **Total Fixed Costs (TFC)**: total obligations of the firm per time period for all fixed inputs

2. **Total Variable Costs (TVC)**: total obligations of the firm per time period for all variable inputs
3. **Total Costs (TC)**: TFC plus TVC

B. **Per-Unit Costs**
1. **Average Fixed Cost (AFC)**: equals total fixed costs divided by output
2. **Average Variable Cost (AVC)**: equals total variable costs divided by output
3. **Average Total Cost (ATC)**: equals total costs divided by output
4. **Marginal Cost (MC)**: equals the change in TC or TVC per unit change in output

C. **Geometry of Per-Unit Cost Curves**
1. The slope of the total cost curve or total variable cost curve derives marginal cost
2. A straight line from the origin to any point on the total cost curve derives average total cost
3. A straight line from the origin to any point on the total variable cost curve derives average variable cost
4. A straight line from the origin to any point on the total fixed cost curve derives average fixed cost

8.3 COST IN THE LONG RUN

A. **Isocost Lines**
1. **Isocost line**: also called the equal-cost line, it shows the various combinations of labor and capital that the firm can hire or rent for the given total cost

B. **Least-Cost Input Combination**: the combination of inputs at the equilibrium point where an isocost line is tangent to an isoquant

C. **Cost Minimization in the Long Run and the Short Run**: in the long run, change both capital and labor and connect separate isoquant-isocost equilibrium points; in the short run, keep one input constant and move to associated equilibrium points and/or where isoquants cross isocost lines

8.4 EXPANSION PATH AND LONG-RUN COST CURVES

A. **Expansion Path and the Long-Run Total Cost Curve**
1. **Expansion path**: joins the origin with the points of tangency of isoquants and the isocost lines
2. **Long-run total cost (LTC) curve**: shows the minimum long-run total costs of producing various levels of output

B. **Derivation of the Long-Run Average and Marginal Cost Curve**
1. **Long-run average cost (LAC)**: curve derived from the LTC curve in the same way as the short-run average total cost (SATC) curve is derived from the short-run total cost (STC) curve
2. **Long-run marginal cost (LMC)**: curve given by the slope of the LTC curve

C. The Relationship Between Short- and Long-Run Average Cost Curves

1. The LAC curve is the tangent to the SATC curves and shows the minimum cost of producing each level of output; mathematically, the LAC is the "envelope" to the SATC curves
2. The LAC curve shows the minimum per-unit cost of producing any level of output when the firm can build any desired scale of plant
3. **The planning horizon**: another term for the long run, it is when the firm has time to build the plant that minimizes the cost of producing any anticipated level of output

8.5 SHAPE OF THE LONG-RUN AVERAGE COST CURVE

1. The LAC is U-shaped due to increasing and decreasing returns to scale
2. Empirical studies seem to indicate that in many industries the LAC curve has a very shallow bottom or is nearly L-shaped, meaning that economies of scale are quickly exhausted and constant returns to scale prevail over a considerable range of output
3. The **minimum efficient scale (MES)** is the smallest quantity at which the LAC curve reaches its minimum

8.6 MULTIPRODUCT FIRMS AND DYNAMIC CHANGES IN COSTS

A. Economies of Scope

1. **Economies of scope**: present when it is cheaper for a single firm to produce various products jointly than for separate firms to produce the same products independently
2. **Diseconomies of scope**: when it is less expensive to produce two products independently than jointly
3. Economies of scope are different than economies of scale; there is no direct relationship between the two

B. The Learning Curve: shows the decline in the average input cost of production with rising cumulative total outputs over time

---

⌘ AT THE FRONTIER ⌘
MINIMIZING COSTS INTERNATIONALLY—THE NEW ECONOMIES OF SCALE

These new economies result from using sources of cheaper inputs and overseas production in order to remain competitive in today's global economy.

PART III: KEY CONCEPTS IN THIS CHAPTER

1. _____ costs require the payment of funds.
2. A(n) _____ shows the various combinations of labor and capital that the firm can hire or rent for the given total costs.

3. The quantities of inputs that result from the equilibrium point where the isocost line is tangent to an isoquant are called the _____ input combination.

4. The costs that do not vary as production is increased or decreased are _____ costs, which constitute the amount paid to the firm's _____ inputs.

5. A firm will hire more _____ inputs in order to raise production, thereby increasing its total _____ costs.

6. When the firm does not produce at all, its total costs are equal to its total _____ costs, since its total _____ costs are zero. Generally, the total costs are the sum of the total _____ costs and the total _____ costs.

7. The total _____ costs are the price of the variable inputs times the quantity purchased of those inputs.

8. The additional costs associated with increased production are called the _____ costs.

9. The marginal costs increase when the _____ marginal returns set in. This means that the marginal costs and the marginal physical product are **directly/inversely** related.

10. The law of diminishing marginal returns stems from the fact that, as the firm hires additional units of _____ inputs to raise production, eventually an additional unit of the input will cause _____ to expand by less than the previous unit did.

11. When the marginal cost is below the average total cost, it must be that the average total costs are _____. When the marginal cost is above the average total cost it must be that the average total costs are _____.

12. We can infer from the previous question that the marginal cost equals the average total cost when the average total cost is at its _____.

13. A firm with one variable input, labor, hires 50 workers to produce 5 units of good Zela. Labor is paid $10 per unit, and the firm has a total cost (TC) of $520. If the firm decides not to produce, its TC would be _____: such a cost would be incurred because the firm would have purchased some inputs that are _____.

14. The law of diminishing marginal returns is applicable in the _____ run, while the question of scaling up is relevant in the _____ run. Geometrically, the _____ path, which is a _____-run notion, is obtained by joining the origin with the points of tangency of isoquants and isocost lines.

15. The long-run _____ cost is the long-run total costs divided by output, while the long-run _____ cost is the additional total costs divided by the expanded output.

16. The long-run average cost curve incorporates the lowest short-run _____ curve for any given level of output. The long-run _____ cost curve shows the lowest unit cost at which a firm can produce various output levels.

17. When the long-run average cost curve slopes downward, the firm is experiencing _____ returns to scale.

18. The lowering of costs that a firm often experiences when it produces two or more products together rather than each alone is called economies of _____, whereas the lowering of costs that a firm often experiences when it expands its production by building additional plants is called economies of _____.

19. The _____ shows the decline in the average input cost of production with rising cumulative total outputs over time.

20. The _____ is the smallest quantity at which the LAC curve reaches its minimum.

PART IV: MULTIPLE-CHOICE QUESTIONS

___1. The actual out-of-pocket expenditures of the firm to purchase or hire inputs it requires in production are the:
   a. real costs of production.
   b. implicit costs.
   c. explicit costs.
   d. opportunity costs.

___2. The isocost line in cost analysis is analogous to the _____ in consumer choice analysis.
   a. budget line
   b. indifference curve
   c. isoquant
   d. demand curve

___3. The total obligations of the firm per time period for all non-variable inputs are the _____ of production.
   a. total cost (TC)
   b. total variable cost (TVC)
   c. opportunity costs
   d. total fixed costs (TFC)

___4. An expansion path is derived by connecting:
   a. points of disequilibrium to points of equilibrium in an Edgeworth box.
   b. equilibrium points as the price of a single input is changed.
   c. equilibrium points as total cost outlays are changed at constant input prices.
   d. equilibrium points as supply and demand curves of non-price variables change.

___5. When a firm benefits from lower costs when it produces two or more products together rather than alone there are:
   a. diminishing returns from producing any single good, but not for all.
   b. economies of scale.
   c. economies of scope.
   d. increasing marginal rates of substitution for all goods.

___6. If it takes fewer hours to produce the last unit of output than it took to produce the first unit of output, then the:
   a. average variable cost per unit of output increases
   b. learning curve indicates a decrease in average input cost of production.
   c. learning curve has a positive slope.
   d. average total cost increases at a decreasing rate.

___7. The major reason for domestic firms foreign "sourcing" of inputs is to:
   a.   remain competitive.
   b.   maximize profits.
   c.   maximize revenues.
   d.   maximize market share.

___8. If non-constant, long-run average cost (LAC) is minimized at $3.25 at output (Q) of 20,000 units, then:
   a.   long-run marginal cost (LMC) is minimized at the same level of output (Q).
   b.   short-run marginal cost (SMC) for the plant size associated with Q = 20,000 is above LAC.
   c.   short-run average total cost (SAC) for the plant size associated with Q = 20,000 is below LAC.
   d.   LAC = LMC = SMC = SAC.

Use the following data to answer questions 9 - 13:

Output	Average Total Cost	Average Fixed Cost
1	$22.00	$2.00
2	$12.00	$1.00
3	$8.66	$0.66
4	$7.00	$0.50

___9. Total fixed cost (TFC) is:
   a. $4.13.
   b. $20.00.
   c. $2.00.
   d. $24.00.

___10. The total cost (TC) of producing 4 units of output is:
   a. $.750.
   b. $6.50.
   c. $69.50.
   d. $28.00.

___11. The total variable cost (TVC) of producing 2 units of output is:
   a. $11.00.
   b. $22.00.
   c. $13.00.
   d. $20.00.

___12. The marginal cost (MC) of increasing output from 1 to 2 units is:
   a. $34.00.
   b. $3.00.
   c. $10.00.
   d. $2.00.

___13. The average variable cost (AVC) of producing 3 units of output is:
   a. $8.00.
   b. $24.00.
   c. $8.66.
   d. $0.66.

___14. For a firm to retain any input in production, it must include as a cost what the input could earn in its best alternative use. This is the _____ doctrine.
   a. alternative or opportunity cost
   b. explicit cost
   c. accounting cost
   d. imaginary cost

___15. If the marginal product of labor (MP_L) is equal to 10, the price of labor (w) is $1.00, the marginal product of capital (MP_K) is 20, and the price of capital (r) is $5.00, then the firm should:
   a. use more capital since the $MP_K > MP_L$.
   b. use less labor because w < r.
   c. use more labor since the MP per dollar spent on labor is greater than that for capital.
   d. do nothing because the firm is in equilibrium where output is maximized for a given total cost.

___16. Which of the following is true of fixed costs?
   a. Average fixed cost (AFC) is constant.
   b. Total fixed costs (TFC) decline as output increases.
   c. The AFC curve touches the horizontal axis at an output close to infinity.
   d. Changes in fixed costs do not cause changes in marginal cost (MC).

___17. If labor (L) is the variable input and capital (K) is the fixed input, and the average product of labor (AP_L) is 25 and the price of labor (w) is $100.00, then the average variable cost (AVC) is:
   a. $0.25.
   b. $2500.00.
   c. $4.00.
   d. equal to marginal cost if w is constant.

___18. When one derives the long-run total cost (LTC) curve using isocost-isoquant analysis:
   a. an envelope of short-run average total cost curves are connected.
   b. points of equilibrium along an expansion path are used.
   c. labor use is varied while holding capital constant.
   d. the LTC curve is a straight line because the expansion path is a straight line.

___19. Empirical studies seem to indicate that in many industries the long-run total cost (LTC) curve:
   a. is nearly "L" shaped.

    b. falls to zero at output equal to infinity.

    c. does not exist.

    d. increases to infinity at output equal to infinity.

___20. If a learning curve indicates that at output $Q_1 = 50$ the short-run average total cost (ATC_1) is equal to $20.00 and at $Q_2 = 30$ $ATC_2 = 25.00, then the long-run average cost (LAC) curve:

    a. does not exist.

    b. has shifted up.

    c. has a slope of zero.

    d. has a slope of infinity.

___21. The social costs are:

    a. explicit costs plus implicit costs.

    b. higher than private costs when a firm does not clean up its pollution.

    c. private costs minus implicit costs.

    d. accounting costs plus opportunity costs.

___22. When capital (K) is placed on the vertical axis and labor (L) on the horizontal axis:

    a. the vertical axis intercept of the isocost line is total costs (TC) divided by the price of labor (w).

    b. the isocost line is $K = L$.

    c. the horizontal axis intercept of the isocost line is TC/r, where r is the price of capital.

    d. the slope of the isocost line is equal to $(-w/r)$.

___23. At equilibrium the marginal rate of technical substitution of labor for capital $(MRTS_{LK})$ is equal to the slope of the:

    a. isocost line, $(-r/w)$.

    b. indifference curve, MU_X/MU_Y.

    c. isoquant, $MP_L/MP_K = w/r$.

    d. budget line, P_X/P_Y.

___24. If capital (K) is the variable input, and labor (L) the fixed input, and the marginal product of capital (MP_K) is 100, and the price of capital (r) is $25.00, then the average variable cost (AVC) is:

    a. $0.25.

    b. $75.00.

    c. $4.00.

    d. $2500.00.

___25. If average total cost (ATC) is $60.00, average variable cost is $40.00, and marginal cost (MC) is $15, then:

    a. ATC is constant and AVC is falling; therefore, output (Q) should be increased.

    b. ATC is increasing and AVC is rising; therefore, output (Q) should be decreased.

    c. AFC is constant at $20.00 for all Q levels.

    d. ATC and AVC are falling; therefore, Q should be increased.

Use Figure 8-1 to answer questions 26 - 30:

FIGURE 8-1

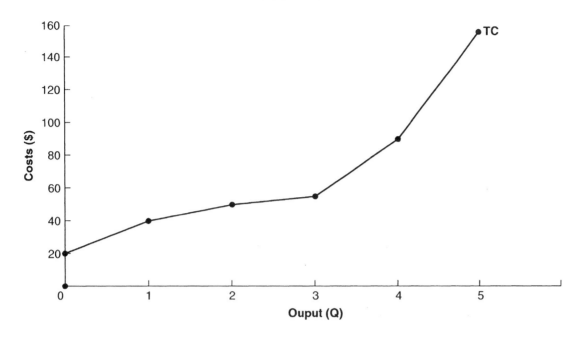

____26. Total fixed cost (TFC) is:
    a. \$20.00 at output $Q_1 = 0$ and \$40.00 at $Q_2 = 1$.
    b. \$20.00 at every level of Q.
    c. equal to total variable cost (TVC) = \$20.00 at Q_1.
    d. equal to infinity at Q > 5.

____27. Total variable cost (TVC):
    a. is zero at Q = 0.
    b. is equal to TFC = \$20.00 at Q = 0.
    c. is equal to total cost (TC) = \$20.00 at Q = 0.
    d. falls as Q increases.

____28. Total cost (TC) is:
    a. zero at Q = 0.
    b. TVC - TFC at every Q level.
    c. TFC + TVC at every Q level.
    d. average total cost (ATC) plus average fixed cost (AFC) at every Q level.

____29. The average fixed cost (AFC) at Q = 4 is:
    a. \$90.00.
    b. \$70.00.
    c. \$20.00.
    d. \$5.00.

___30. The marginal cost (MC) of changing from Q = 1 to Q = 2 is:
  a. $40.00.
  b. $50.00.
  c. $10.00.
  d. $20.00.

CHAPTER 9:

PRICE AND OUTPUT
UNDER PERFECT COMPETITION

Prior to reading chapter 9, match statements at left with the appropriate concept at right.

___1. Highest benefits forfeited when an action is taken
___2. Horizontal summation of individual demand curves
___3. Total cost minus total fixed cost
___4. Total cost divided by output
___5. Additional cost incurred as firm increases production
___6. Total fixed costs per unit produced
___7. A change in the quantity demanded due to changing tastes
___8. Situation where markets clear
___9. Price times quantity sold
___10. Higher costs of production
___11. Price minus average total cost
___12. Total explicit plus implicit costs
___13. Shows the various combinations of labor and capital that
      the firm can hire or rent for the given total costs

a. average total cost
b. total revenues
c. marginal costs
d. demand shift
e. average fixed cost
f. opportunity cost
g. upward shift of
   cost curves
h. market demand
i. equilibrium
j. per unit profit
k. total variable cost
l. isocost line
m. total costs

9.1   MARKET STRUCTURE: PERFECT COMPETITION
1. **Perfect competition**: the type of market organization in which:
    a. there are many buyers and sellers of a commodity, each too small to affect the price of the commodity
    b. the commodity is homogeneous
    c. there is perfect mobility of resources
    d. economic agents have perfect knowledge of market conditions
2. The perfectly competitive model provides the point of reference or standard against which to measure the economic cost or inefficiency of departures from perfect competition
3. Under perfect competition the firm is a price taker and can sell any quantity of the commodity at the given market price

4. The perfectly competitive firm faces a horizontal or infinitely elastic demand curve at the price determined at the intersection of the market demand and supply curves for the commodity

9.2 PRICE DETERMINATION IN THE MARKET PERIOD
1. **Market period**: period of time during which no input can be varied and so the market supply of a commodity is fixed.

9.3 SHORT-RUN EQUILIBRIUM OF THE FIRM
A. **Total Approach**: Maximizing the Positive Difference Between Total Revenue and Total Costs
1. Total profits are maximized when the positive difference between total revenue and total costs is largest
2. **Break-even point**: where total revenue equals total cost
B. **Marginal Approach**: Equating Marginal Revenue and Marginal Cost
1. The firm is in short-run equilibrium or maximizes total profits by producing the output where marginal revenue (slope of total revenue) is equal to marginal cost (slope of total cost) and marginal cost is rising
C. **Profit Maximization or Loss Minimization?**
1. At the best or optimum level of output (the output level at which MR = MC and MC is rising) the firm can make a profit, break even, or incur a loss.
2. As long as the price (P) exceeds the average variable cost (AVC) it pays the firm to produce, because by doing so it would minimize its losses
3. **Shut down point**: the point where price equals average variable cost; the firm is indifferent between producing or shutting down because in either case it would incur a loss equal to its fixed costs

9.4 SHORT-RUN SUPPLY CURVE AND EQUILIBRIUM
A. **Short-Run Supply Curve of the Firm and Industry**
1. The perfectly competitive firm's short-run supply curve is its marginal cost curve above minimum point on average variable cost curve (i.e., above the shut down point).
2. **The industry short-run supply curve** is the horizontal summation of the supply curves of all the firms in the industry
3. **Price elasticity of supply**: measures the responsiveness or sensitivity in the quantity supplied of a commodity to a change in price
B. **Short-Run Equilibrium of the Industry and Firm**
a. The intersection of the industry supply and demand curves determines the level of the horizontal demand curve facing the individual firm
b. The intersection of that horizontal demand curve (which is also the marginal revenue curve) and the firm's marginal cost curve then determines the firm's best level of output

9.5 LONG-RUN EQUILIBRIUM OF THE FIRM AND INDUSTRY
A. **Long-Run Equilibrium of the Firm**: in the long run, all inputs are variable and the firm can build the most efficient plant (lowest possible cost) to produce

the best or most profitable level of output (the output at which P = MR = LMC and LMC is rising)
  B. **Long-Run Equilibrium of the Industry and Firm**
    1. The industry (and the firm) will be in long-run equilibrium when the price is at a level such that all firms make zero economic profits (they break even or earn only a normal return)
    2. If economic profits were positive, entry would occur, meaning the industry is not in equilibrium
    3. In long-run equilibrium P = MR = LMC = SMC = LAC = SATC
  C. **Efficiency Implications of Perfect Competition**
    1. Resources are used most efficiently to produce the goods and services most desired by society at the minimum cost
    2. Distributional efficiency: since P = LAC, the perfectly competitive firm earns zero profits in the long run
    3. Production efficiency: since P = LMC, each firm produces at the lowest point on the LAC curve

9.6   CONSTANT, INCREASING, AND DECREASING COST INDUSTRIES
  A. **Constant Cost Industries**
    1. **Constant cost industry**: if input prices remain constant, the new long-run equilibrium price for the commodity will be the same as before the increase in demand and supply
    2. The long-run industry supply curve is horizontal at the minimum LAC
  B. **Increasing Cost Industries**
    1. **Increasing cost industry**: if input prices rise as more inputs are demanded by an expanding industry, the firms' cost curves will shift up
    2. The long-run industry supply curve for the commodity will be positively sloped
    3. **External diseconomy**: upward shift in the firm's per-units cost curves as the industry expands
  C. **Decreasing Cost Industries**
    1. **Decreasing cost industry**: if input prices fall as more inputs are demanded by an expanding industry, the firms' cost curve will shift down
    2. The long-run industry supply curve for the commodity will be negatively sloped
    3. **External economy**: downward shift in the firm's per-unit cost curves as the industry expands

9.7   **INTERNATIONAL COMPETITION IN THE DOMESTIC ECONOMY**: allows consumers to purchase more of a commodity at a lower price than in the absence of imports

9.8 ANALYSIS OF COMPETITIVE MARKETS

A. Producer Surplus: excess of the commodity price over the marginal cost of production and is measured by the area between the commodity price and producer's marginal cost curve

B. Consumers' and Producers' Surplus, and the Efficiency of Perfect Competition: combined consumers' and producers' surplus is maximum when supply curve intersects demand curve in a perfectly competitive market

C. The Welfare Effects of an Excise Tax
   1. **Deadweight loss**: net loss in consumers' and producers' surplus due to excise tax

D. The Effects of an Import Tariff: results in a deadweight loss

---

⌘ AT THE FRONTIER ⌘
AUCTIONING AIRWAVES

Between December 1994 and March 1995, the U.S. Government auctioned off to the highest bidder thousands of licenses to offer new personal communication services (PCS) for $7.7 billion.

PART III: KEY CONCEPTS IN THIS CHAPTER

1. A perfectly competitive market is the type of market organization in which there are **many/few** buyers and sellers of a commodity, each too **small/large** to affect the price of the commodity. This means that all firms are price **takers/makers**.

2. A perfectly competitive market is the type of market organization in which: (1) the commodity is _____; (2) there is a perfect _____ of resources; and (3) economic agents have _____ of market conditions.

3. The period of time during which the market supply of a commodity is fixed is called _____ period.

4. _____ are the difference between the total revenues and the total costs; the point at which that difference is zero is called the _____ point.

5. Losses are minimized when the _____ equals the _____. In spite of losses, the firm will continue to operate as long as the price covers the _____ costs.

6. The output level at which the perfectly competitive firm maximizes its profits happens to be the one where the price equals the **marginal revenues/marginal costs/average revenues/demand/all of the above**.

7. If a perfectly competitive firm increases its price above the market price, it will lose a **small/large** share of its customers to competing firms. The firm's demand is perfectly **elastic/inelastic** meaning that it is **vertical/horizontal**.

8. The supply curve for a perfectly competitive firm is its _____ curve above the shut down point.

9.   Suppose that the market price is $10. From this information, we can calculate (estimate) the firm's **marginal revenue/average revenue/demand/all of the above/none of the above**.

10.   Suppose that the market price is $10. From this information we can calculate the firm's **marginal cost/average cost/average variable cost/all of the above/none of the above**.

Consider the following data for questions 11 – 13: equilibrium price is $10, quantity produced and sold is 100 units, average total cost is $9, and the average variable cost is $6.

11.   From this information, we can conclude that the total revenues are $_____, the total cost is $_____, and the total fixed cost is $_____. The firm is making $_____ total profits.

12.   From this information, we can conclude that the marginal revenues are $_____, the average revenues are $_____, while the marginal costs are **$10/impossible to determine** (since we do not know whether the firm is maximizing its profits or not).

13.   From this information and knowing that the total cost of producing 101 units is $915 while that of producing 99 units is $895, we can conclude that the firm ought to expand/contract/keep constant its production.

14.   The _____ curve is the horizontal sum of the portion of the marginal cost curves above the point where P = AVC of all firms in the industry.

15.   If a typical firm earns positive economic profits, _____ will likely occur raising the _____ of the good thereby decreasing the _____ of the good and eliminating all economic profits in the _____-run.

16.   In the long-run competitive equilibrium, the typical firm's economic profit is _____. The long-run competitive equilibrium is characterized by a price equaling **SAC/LAC/SMC/LMC/AR/MR/all of the above/none of the above**.

17.   As the demand for residential construction rises, the demand for lumber rises, thereby raising the price of lumber. Hence, residential construction is a(n) _____ cost industry.

18.   If an increase in the demand for inputs causes their price to decline, then the industry is a(n) _____ cost industry which will see its average total cost curve shift _____.

19.   In a decreasing cost industry an increase in demand will cause the market price to _____ in the long run due to the firm's realization of _____ economies.

20.   The _____ of perfect competition stems from the fact that consumers' and producers' surplus is maximum when the supply curve _____ the demand curve.

PART IV: MULTIPLE-CHOICE QUESTIONS

____1. Which of the following is not a characteristic of perfect competition?
    a.   many buyers and sellers
    b.   the commodity is homogeneous

    c.   there is perfect mobility of resources

    d.   the firm faces a downward sloped demand curve

____2. In the market period:

    a.   the supply curve is perpendicular to the horizontal axis and parallel to the vertical axis.

    b.   the supply curve is perpendicular to the vertical axis and parallel to the horizontal axis.

    c.   the demand curve has a slope of zero and a price elasticity of demand (η) of infinity.

    d.   the demand curve has a slope of infinity and a price elasticity of demand (η) of zero.

Use the following information to answer questions 3 – 5:

Suppose there is a perfectly competitive firm with minimum marginal cost (MC) of $5 at output (Q) of 3, minimum average variable cost (AVC) of $7 at Q = 4, and minimum average total cost (ATC) of $9 at Q = 5. In all cases, costs rise after the indicated Q levels.

____3. The firm's shut down point is:

    a.   at Q = 5, since at Q levels less than 5 the firm is incurring a loss.

    b.   at Q = 3, since economic decisions are made with marginal values.

    c.   at Q = 4, since the rational producer will only operate when P > minimum AVC.

    d.   not possible to calculate, since nothing is revealed regarding revenue.

____4. The firm's overall single point break-even point is:

    a.   at Q = 3, since marginal revenue (MR) will also be $5.

    b.   at Q = 5, since price (P), average revenue (AR) and marginal revenue (MR) will also be $9.

    c.   at Q = 4, since it is rational to produce at all Q levels equal to or greater than 4.

    d.   not possible to calculate, since nothing is revealed regarding revenue.

____5. The firm's supply curve is measured by the:

    a.   marginal cost (MC) curve between Q = 3 and Q = 4, since it is rational to produce at a loss in this region.

    b.   marginal cost (MC) curve at Q = 3, since the firm is above to pay off more than average variable cost (AVC) in this region.

    c.   marginal cost (MC) curve at Q = 4, since the firm will be making a positive accounting profit in this region.

    d.   not possible to calculate, since nothing is revealed regarding revenue.

____6. The profit maximizing level of output (Q) of the firm in the long run in perfect competition is:

    a.   never the same as the profit maximizing level of Q of the firm in the short run.

    b.   at Q levels less than that associated with minimum long-run average total cost (LAC).

    c.   at whichever price or marginal revenue equals long-run marginal cost (LMC).

    d.   never the same as the most efficient plant.

___7. A constant cost industry is one for which:
   a. input prices are bid up as the industry expands.
   b. the slope of the long-run supply curve is negative.
   c. the slope of the long-run supply curve is zero.
   d. input prices are bid down as the industry expands.

___8. If the foreign supply curve (S_f) of a nation's imports of commodity X has a positive slope:
   a. then domestic consumption will be more than if S_f had a slope of zero.
   b. the imports would be more than if S_f had a slope of zero.
   c. then a tariff would result in lower prices for commodity X.
   d. the imports would be less than if S_f had a slope of zero.

___9. If marginal cost (MC) is equal to the price (P) of $10 (given off a horizontal demand curve) at output level (Q) of 8 units, and if the straight line MC curve intersects the vertical axis at $2, the producer surplus is:
   a. $80, since P(Q) = $10(8) = $80.
   b. $32, since [($10 - $2)8][0.5] = $8(8)0.5 = $64(0.5) = $32.
   c. $64, since ($10 - $2)8 = $8(8) = $64.
   d. not possible to calculate, since nothing is revealed regarding revenue.

___10. Under perfect competition, the firm:
   a. is a price taker and can sell any quantity of the commodity at the given market price.
   b. is a price maker since the industry demand curve has a negative slope.
   c. can charge any price it wants.
   d. can withhold supply from the market and drive price up.

___11. The total approach to profit maximization indicates that:
   a. at output (Q) zero, total revenue (TR) exceeds short-run total cost (STC) by the amount of total fixed cost (TFC).
   b. if the STC curve reflects a total product (TP) curve that is downward sloping, then there will be only one break-even point or none at all.
   c. if the STC curve reflects a total product (TP) curve that is upward sloping, then there will be only one break-even point or none at all.
   d. total profits are maximized when the positive difference between total revenue (TR) and short-run total costs (STC) is largest.

___12. In perfect competition, the industry supply curve is:
   a. the horizontal sum of the individual marginal cost (MC) curves, each of which is made up of the locus points at which MC = MR above the minimum points on their respective average variable cost (AVC) curves.
   b. the vertical sum of the individual marginal cost (MC) curves, each of which is made up of the locus points at which MC = MR above the minimum points on their respective average variable cost (AVC) curves.
   c. measured from the point of origin.

    d.   not possible to calculate, because downward sloping supply curves make unique MC = MR equilibrium points impossible.

___13. In perfect competition, if the lowest short-run average total cost (SAC) curve yields a minimum SAC = $3.25 at output (Q) of 55, then in the long run:
    a.   P = AR = MR = SMC = SAC = LMC = LAC = $3.25 at Q = 55.
    b.   The price (P) must be greater than $3.25 at Q = 55.
    c.   P = AR = MR = SMC = SAC = LMC = LAC = $3.25 at Q < 55.
    d.   P = AR = MR = SMC = SAC = LMC = LAC = $3.25 at Q > 55.

___14. If the long-run supply curve has a positive slope, then there is:
    a.   a constant cost industry, since input prices are constant as demand changes.
    b.   a decreasing cost industry, since input prices decrease as demand increases.
    c.   an increasing cost industry, since input prices increase as demand increases.
    d.   no implication for constant, decreasing, nor increasing cost industries.

___15. If a straight line demand curve has a vertical axis intercept of $18, and if a straight line supply curve has a vertical axis intercept of $2, and if equilibrium results in price (P) of $10 and quantity (Q) of 8 units, then:
    a.   consumers' surplus is zero.
    b.   producers' surplus is ($10 - $2)8 = $8(8) = $64.
    c.   consumers' surplus is ($10 - $2)8 = $8(8) = $64.
    d.   the sum of consumers' surplus ($18 - $10)(8)(0.5) = $32 plus producers' surplus ($10 - $2)(8)(0.5) = $32 equals $64.

___16. As an industry expands, the effect of an external economy is a(n) _____ shift in the firm's per-unit cost curves due to a(n) _____ in input prices.
    a.   upward, increase
    b.   upward, decrease
    c.   downward, increase
    d.   downward, decrease

___17. In the long run, the most efficient plant is one:
    a.   at which output (Q) is increasing, because marginal revenue (MR) is greater than marginal cost (MC).
    b.   at which output (Q) is decreasing, because marginal revenue (MR) is less than marginal cost (MC).
    c.   that allows the firm to produce MR = MC at the lowest possible cost.
    d.   that does not necessarily produce the best level of output (Q).

___18. If the market demand increases due to an increase in average consumer income, and if the market supply curve is upward sloping, then the firm's ____ demand curve will shift _____.
    a.   horizontal, down
    b.   horizontal, up
    c.   vertical, right
    d.   vertical, left

Use the following information to answer questions 19 – 23:
In the short run for a perfectly competitive firm, assume that average total cost (ATC) is $50, average variable cost (AVC) is $30, marginal cost (MC) is $40, marginal revenue (MR) is $40, all at output (Q) of 25.

___19. Average profit is:
   a. -$10, since P = MR = $40 and ATC is $50.
   b. -$250, since TC = $1250 and TR = $1000.
   c. $50
   d. $40

___20. The shut down point is at:
   a. Q = 25.
   b. Q < 25.
   c. Q > 25.
   d. Unable to determine with the information provided.

___21. The single overall break-even point is at:
   a. Q = 25.
   b. Q < 25.
   c. Q > 25.
   d. Unable to determine with the information provided.

___22. If MR were to rise to $60 at Q = 30 with new ATC = $55 and AVC = $45, then:
   a. MR = MC would no longer hold.
   b. the firm would still be in the region where AVC < P < ATC.
   c. the firm would break even.
   d. an average profit of $5 would be earned.

___23. If MR were to fall to $35 at Q = 20 with new ATC = $53 and AVC = $41, then:
   a. the firm would still be in the region where AVC < P < ATC.
   b. the firm would shut down since P < AVC.
   c. MR = MR would no longer hold.
   d. the firm would break even.

___24. If the commodity is identical or perfectly standardized so that the output (Q) of each producer is indistinguishable from that of the other producers, then the commodity is:
   a. homogeneous.
   b. heterogeneous.
   c. not perfectly substitutable.
   d. a Giffen good.

___25. The efficient-market hypothesis applies most closely to:
   a. stocks.
   b. goods imported or exported.
   c. the labor market for government agents.
   d. all goods and services.

Use Figure 9-1 to answer questions 26 – 30:

FIGURE 9-1

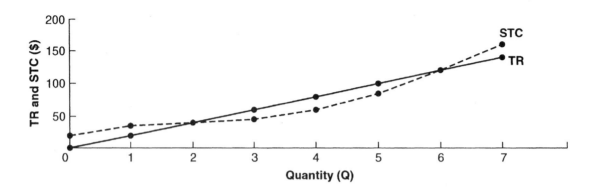

_____26. Profits are maximized at:
   a. Q = 0.
   b. Q = 2.
   c. Q = 4.
   d. Q = 6.

_____27. Where is the short-run total cost (STC) minimized?
   a. Q = 0
   b. Q = 2
   c. Q = 4
   d. Q = 6

_____28. Where are the break-even points?
   a. Q = 0 and Q = infinity
   b. Q = 2 and Q = 6
   c. Q = 2 only
   d. Q = 6 only

_____29. Which output (Q) is associated with a total profit curve with slope equal to zero?
   a. Q = 0
   b. Q = 2
   c. Q = 4
   d. Q = 6

_____30. Which outputs are associated with a total profit curve touching its horizontal axis?
   a. Q = 0 and Q = infinity
   b. Q = 2 and Q = 6
   c. Q = 2 only
   d. Q = 4 only

CHAPTER 10:

PRICE AND OUTPUT UNDER PURE MONOPOLY

PART I: REVIEW OF CONCEPTS FROM PREVIOUS CHAPTER

Prior to reading chapter 10, match statements at left with the appropriate concept at right.

____1. Total revenues minus total costs

____2. Horizontal summation of individual demand curves

____3. Per-unit cost, meaning TC/Q

____4. Measure of responsiveness of consumers to price changes

____5. TVC/Q

____6. Losses cause the firm to _____ in the long run.

____7. Profit maximizing rule

____8. Two goods that satisfy the same wants

____9. Additional cost incurred in order to raise output

____10. New firms begin supplying a good

____11. Industry where all sellers are price takers

____12. Extra revenue generated by selling additional quantities

____13. Upward shift in the firm's LAC curve as industry expands

____14. Excess of commodity price over the marginal cost of production

a. elasticity of demand

b. entry

c. marginal cost

d. marginal revenue

e. MR = MC

f. SATC

g. profits

h. perfect competition

i. substitutes

j. market demand

k. AVC

l. exit

m. producers' surplus

n. external diseconomy

PART II: ANNOTATED CHAPTER OUTLINE

10.1 PURE MONOPOLY—THE OPPOSITE EXTREME FROM PERFECT COMPETITION

A. Definition and Sources of Monopoly

1. **Pure monopoly**: form of market organization in which a single firm sells a commodity for which there are no close substitutes

   a. A monopolist can earn profits in the long run because entry into the industry is blocked or very difficult

   b. Monopoly can arise because a firm owns or controls the entire supply of a raw material required in the production of a commodity or possesses some unique managerial talent, or as a result of patents giving the firm exclusive rights to produce a commodity or use a particular production process

   c. Some monopolies are created by government franchises

2. **Natural monopoly**: single firm supplying the entire market
   a. Natural monopoly is the result of economies of scale operating over a sufficiently large range of outputs
B. **The Monopolist Faces the Market Demand Curve for the Commodity**
   1. As the sole seller of a commodity the monopolist faces the negatively sloped industry demand curve for the commodity.
   2. To sell more units of the commodity the monopolist must lower the commodity price.
   3. As a result, MR < P and the marginal revenue curve lies below the demand curve

10.2 SHORT-RUN EQUILIBRIUM PRICE AND OUTPUT
A. **Total Approach: Maximizing the Positive Difference Between Total Revenue and Total Costs**
   1. Maximum profit where the positive difference between the TR and STC curves is greatest
B. **Marginal Approach**: Equating Marginal Revenue and Marginal Cost
   1. Maximum profits at the level of output where marginal revenue equals marginal cost
C. **Profit Maximization or Loss Minimization?**
   1. Profits are not guaranteed where marginal costs equal marginal revenue, just the maximum profit or minimum loss
   2. The monopolist will produce at a loss as long as it can cover its AVC and part of its AFC
   3. At P = AVC the monopolist would be indifferent between producing or shutting down, because either way its loss would equal its fixed cost. This is the monopolist's shut down point
D. **Short-Run Marginal Cost and Supply**
   1. The monopolist's short-run supply curve is NOT the rising portion of its marginal cost (MC) curve over the average variable cost (AVC) curve
   2. This is because the monopolist could supply the same quantity of output at different prices depending on the price elasticity of demand; thus there is no unique relationship between price and quantity supplied, so no supply curve

10.3 LONG-RUN EQUILIBRIUM PRICE AND OUTPUT
A. **Profit Maximization in the Long Run**
   1. In the long run all inputs are variable and the monopolist can build the most efficient plant to produce the best level of output
   2. The monopolist will produce the level of output at which marginal revenue equals long-run marginal cost, and will build the plant represented by the SATC curve tangent to the LAC curve at that level of output
B. **Comparison with Perfect Competition: The Social Cost of Monopoly**
   1. Price is higher and quantity is less with monopoly than in perfect competition

10.4 PROFIT MAXIMIZATION BY THE MULTIPLANT MONOPOLIST

A. **Short-Run Equilibrium**: produce in each plant where the marginal cost of the last unit of output is equal to the marginal revenue from selling the combined output of all plants

B. **Long-Run Equilibrium:** build as many identical plants of optimal size as are required to produce the best level of output, where the best level of output is given by LMC = MR

10.5   PRICE DISCRIMINATION—A MONOPOLIST'S METHOD OF INCREASING PROFITS Price discrimination is the charging of different prices for different quantities of a commodity or in different markets, which are not justified by cost differences

A. **Charging Different Prices for Different Quantities**

1. **First degree or perfect price discrimination**: sell each unit of the commodity separately and charge the highest price each consumer would be willing to pay for the commodity rather than go without it; the monopolist is thus able to exact the entire consumers' surplus from consumers

2. **Second degree or multipart price discrimination**: charging of a uniform price per unit for a specific quantity of the commodity, a lower price per unit for an additional batch or block of the commodity, and so on. The monopolist is thus able to exact part of the consumers' surplus from consumers

B. **Charging Different Prices in Different Markets**

1. **Third degree price discrimination**: charging a different price in different markets

2. The monopolist will sell at a higher price in the market with the more inelastic demand

3. For the firm to be able to practice third degree price discrimination, three conditions must be met:

    a. the firm must have some monopoly power

    b. the firm must be able to keep the two markets separate, so as to avoid arbitrage

    c. the price elasticity of demand must be different in the two markets

10.6   INTERNATIONAL PRICE DISCRIMINATION AND DUMPING

1. **Dumping**: international price discrimination; the charging of a lower price abroad than at home for the same commodity

    a. **Persistent dumping**: result of international price discrimination

    b. **Predatory dumping**: temporary sale of a commodity at below cost or at a lower price abroad in order to drive foreign producers out of business, after which prices are raised to take advantage of the monopoly power that has been acquired

    c. **Sporadic dumping**: the occasional sale of the commodity at below cost or at a lower price abroad than domestically in order to unload an unforeseen and temporary surplus of a commodity without having to reduce domestic prices

10.5 TWO-PART TARIFFS, TYING, AND BUNDLING
   A. Two-Part Tariffs
   1. **Two-part tariff**: consumers pay an initial fee for the right to purchase a product as well as a usage fee or price for each unit of the product they purchase
   B. Tying and Bundling
   1. **Tying**: requirement that a consumer who buys or leases a monopolist's product also purchase another product needed in the use of the first; often used as a form of a two-part tariff
   2. **Bundling**: a monopolist requires customers buying or leasing one of its products or services to also buy or lease another product or service when customers have different tastes but the monopolist cannot price discriminate (as in tying)

10.6 ANALYSIS OF MONOPOLY MARKETS
   A. Per-Unit Tax: Perfect Competition and Monopoly Compared
   1. A per-unit excise tax will fall entirely on consumers in perfect competition and will fall only partly on consumers in monopoly (if both the monopolist and the perfectly competitive industry operate under conditions of constant costs)
   B. Price Discrimination and the Existence of the Industry: sometimes third degree price discrimination is necessary for a firm to exist; the commodity or service would not be supplied in the long run in the absence of a subsidy
   C. Do Monopolists Suppress Inventions? No, since inventions usually increase profits.

⌘   AT THE FRONTIER   ⌘
MICROSOFT LAUNCHES WINDOWS 95—A SOFTWARE NEAR MONOPOLY LANDS MICROSOFT IN THE COURTS

The introduction of Windows 95 is as close as we come today to a pure monopoly in a major U.S. industry.

PART III: KEY CONCEPTS IN THIS CHAPTER

1. A _____ is a form of market organization in which a single firm sells a commodity for which there are no close substitutes.
2. A _____ is a single firm supplying the entire market, caused by economies of scale operating over a sufficiently large range of outputs.
3. The monopolist faces the _____ curve, which **is/is not** a horizontal, perfectly elastic curve.
4. If a monopolist decreases price to sell another unit, the marginal revenue is _____ than the price charged. This means that the marginal revenue (MR) curve for a monopolist is _____ the demand curve for the product.

5. Producing the best level of output at which marginal cost equals marginal revenue **guarantees/does not guarantee** profits to the monopolist.

6. Suppose the market demand curve for a monopolistic industry is $P = \$22 - Q_d$. The total revenue generated by this monopolist when selling 8 units are \$_____, while the marginal revenue generated when selling the 8th unit is \$_____. The selling price of selling 8 units is \$_____ and is **higher/lower** than the marginal revenue from selling the 8th unit.

7. The supply curve **can/cannot** be derived for a monopoly firm because any selected quantity cannot be associated with a(n) _____ price.

8. Profit maximization in the long run occurs at the quantity where the _____ equals the _____.

9. In the short run, by producing an output where _____ equals _____, the monopolist maximizes profit and charges a price that _____ the marginal cost.

10. In spite of a price that exceeds the marginal revenue, if the price is lower than the SATC, then the monopoly firm is realizing a(n) _____.

11. In order to assess the social cost of a monopoly we compare the long-run equilibrium price and output of a monopoly with that of the perfectly competitive industry and find that the price is _____ and the quantity is _____ with monopoly than in perfect competition.

12. The short-run equilibrium for a profit-maximizing multiplant monopolist is reached when the latter produces in each plant where the _____ of the last unit of output is equal to the _____ from selling the combined output of all plants.

13. The long-run equilibrium for a profit-maximizing multiplant monopolist is reached when the latter operates each of _____ plants where the _____ equals the _____, which equals the _____ and the _____.

14. Charging different prices for different quantities of a commodity or in different markets, which are not justified by cost differences, is called _____.

15. There are _____ degrees of price discrimination. **First/second/third** degree price discrimination consists of extracting the entire consumers' surplus from the consumer.

16. **First/second/third degree** price discrimination consists of charging different prices in different markets. Sometimes third degree price discrimination is _____ for a firm to exist.

17. **First/second/third degree** price discrimination consists of charging a uniform price per unit for a specific quantity of the commodity, and a lower price per unit for an additional batch or block of the commodity.

18. International price discrimination is called _____.

19. The phenomenon of a monopolist requiring customers who buy or lease one of its products or services to also buy or lease another product or service when customers have different tastes but the monopolist cannot price discriminate is called

    _____.

20. A per-unit excise tax will fall entirely on the consumer in a _____ industry and will fall only partly on consumers in a _____ industry.

PART IV: MULTIPLE-CHOICE QUESTIONS

___1. The form of market organization in which a single firm sells a product for which there are no close substitutes is:
   a.   pure monopoly.
   b.   perfect competition.
   c.   homogeneous oligopoly.
   d.   heterogeneous oligopoly.

___2. For a monopolist, the total revenue (TR) curve is:
   a.   always everywhere above the short-run average total cost (SATC) curve.
   b.   always everywhere below the SATC curve.
   c.   a straight line.
   d.   a dome shaped curve.

___3. In the long run, the monopolist maximizes profits where:
   a.   long-run marginal cost (LMC) is minimum.
   b.   the LMC curve intersects the marginal revenue (MR) curve from below.
   c.   the LMC curve crosses the long-run average cost (LAC) curve.
   d.   the short-run average total cost (SATC) is equal to LAC.

___4. The horizontal sum of multiplant monopolist short-run marginal costs (SMC) from each plant equals:
   a.   producers' surplus
   b.   a supply curve for the entire firm.
   c.   SMC for the entire firm.
   d.   short-run average total cost (SATC).

___5. If a monopolist charges $5 in market A and $3.50 in market B for the same good with identical production costs, then:
   a.   the monopolist should sell only to market A.
   b.   there is first degree price discrimination.
   c.   there is second degree price discrimination.
   d.   there is third degree price discrimination.

___6. International price discrimination is called:
   a.   limit pricing.
   b.   dumping.
   c.   transfer pricing.
   d.   two-part pricing.

____7. In two-part pricing, if the vertical axis intercept is $5 and marginal cost (MC) is constant at $1 at quantity (Q) equal to 3 where it intersects a downward sloping straight-line demand curve, then the initial or membership fee would be:
    a. $12.
    b. $4.
    c. $6.
    d. Unable to calculate without marginal revenue (MR) information.

____8. Suppose that a perfectly competitive firm produces 6 units of good X (Q) at a price (P) equal to $3.25. If a monopolist were to produce the same good under identical production costs, then the monopolist would:
    a. set P > $3.25 and have an equilibrium Q < 6.
    b. set P < $3.25 and have an equilibrium Q > 6.
    c. make a lower total profit.
    d. charge the same P and offer the same Q on the market as the perfectly competitive firm.

____9. Bundling by a monopolist is:
    a. a form of tying where different products are sold as a package rather than sold separately.
    b. a form of tying with price discrimination.
    c. the same as limit pricing.
    d. the same as marginal pricing.

____10. Predatory dumping is:
    a. the occasional sale of a commodity at a price below cost.
    b. the same as persistent dumping.
    c. the temporary sale of a commodity below cost or at a lower price abroad to drive foreign producers out of business.
    d. charging a price equal to average revenue.

____11. Under third degree price discrimination, if the price in market one (P_1) is $3.50 at quantity ($Q_1$) equals 2, and price in market two (P_2) is $1.50 at quantity ($Q_2$) equals 1.5, then:
    a. price (P) without price discrimination must be the average of these prices, $2.50.
    b. quantity without price discrimination would be Q > 3.5.
    c. quantity without price discrimination would be Q < 3.5.
    d. price (P) without price discrimination would be $1.50 < P < $3.50.

____12. In the long run, in order to produce larger output, the multiplant monopolist will:
    a. produce in a plant the same size as one in perfect competition.
    b. engage in first degree price discrimination.
    c. hold capital constant and increase the use of labor.
    d. build additional plants identical to those already existing.

___13. If under perfect competition a straight-line market demand curve intersects the vertical axis at $4.50 and hits the horizontal axis at quantity (Q) 4.5, and if a horizontal supply curve results in an equilibrium price (P) of $1.50 and an equilibrium quantity (Q) of 1.5, then the social cost of monopolizing this industry is:
   a. equal to monopoly profits, $2.25.
   b. $(3 - 1.5)(\$3 - \$1.50)(0.5) = \$1.13$, since marginal revenue (MR) equals marginal cost (MC) at Q = 1.5.
   c. ($4.50 - $1.50)(3) = $9.
   d. $(4.50 - \$1.50)(3)(0.5) = \$4.50$.

___14. Under monopoly with an equilibrium at quantity (Q) equal to 1.5 units, the supply curve:
   a. is the short-run average total cost (SATC) curve above the minimum point (above 1.5 units) on the average variable cost curve.
   b. does not exist since there is not a single unique price which can be associated with Q = 1.5.
   c. is the marginal cost (MC) curve.
   d. cannot be determined since no information is given concerning revenue.

___15. For a monopolist with a demand curve that is not infinitely elastic:
   a. price (P) is equal to marginal revenue (MR).
   b. price elasticity of demand (η) is less than infinity, thus MR > P.
   c. price elasticity of demand (η) is less than infinity, thus MR < P.
   d. P < MR regardless of the value of η.

___16. If a monopolist's price (P) is known to be $5.78 in equilibrium, then:
   a. average revenue (AR) is less than $5.78.
   b. marginal cost (MC) is equal to $5.78.
   c. marginal revenue (MR) is equal to $5.78.
   d. MR = MC and both are less than $5.78.

___17. When marginal revenue (MR) is zero, the price elasticity of demand (η) is:
   a. between zero and one.
   b. greater than one.
   c. equal to one.
   d. less than one.

___18. If a monopolist's price (P) is $4.15, average total cost (ATC) is $5.25 and average variable cost (AVC) is $3.75, then the firm would:
   a. go out of business.
   b. stay in business, lose $1.10 per unit of output; it can pay average variable cost plus part of average fixed cost.
   c. operate with a $0.40 per unit profit since P > AVC.
   d. operate with a $0.40 per unit loss since P > AVC.

___19. Under monopoly with an equilibrium price (P) equal to $7.55, the supply curve:
    a. is the short-run average total cost (SATC) curve above the minimum point on the average variable cost curve.
    b. does not exist since there is not a single unique quantity (Q) which can be associated with P = $7.55.
    c. is the marginal cost (MC) curve.
    d. cannot be determined since no information is given concerning revenue.

___20. Why should a consumer care if a perfectly competitive industry is converted into a monopoly?
    a. Part of the consumers' surplus is lost as monopoly profit and as social cost.
    b. Price is lower under monopoly.
    c. Quantity is higher under monopoly.
    d. Monopoly profit and social cost is converted into consumers' surplus.

___21. If a monopolist can sell each unit of a good separately and charge the highest price a consumer is willing to pay rather than go without the good, there is:
    a. first degree or perfect price discrimination.
    b. second degree or multiplant price discrimination.
    c. third degree price discrimination.
    d. fourth-degree price discrimination.

___22. Under third degree price discrimination, the highest price (P) is charged in:
    a. the total market if there were not price discrimination.
    b. the market segment with the relatively elastic demand.
    c. the market segment with the relatively inelastic demand.
    d. Both segments of the market are charged the same price.

___23. Tying refers to requiring consumers to:
    a. pay an initial fee for the right to purchase a product.
    b. pay a usage fee for each unit of the product they purchase.
    c. purchase the full line of products offered by the firm.
    d. purchase another product needed in the use of the first.

___24. For a monopolist, the introduction of an innovation is likely to:
    a. not be made, because profits would likely decrease.
    b. be made, because profits would likely increase.
    c. be made, but inventions are more important.
    d. not be made, since inventions are more important.

_____25. When a per-unit tax is placed on a perfectly competitive firm and compared to a per-unit tax placed on a monopoly firm, assuming both firms have identical horizontal supply and/or marginal cost curves and identical demand curves:
    a. the new equilibrium price is higher for the perfectly competitive firm.
    b. the new equilibrium quantity is lower for the perfectly competitive firm.
    c. the decline in the equilibrium quantity in the monopoly firm is one-half the decline in the perfectly competitive firm.
    d. the decline in the equilibrium quantity in the monopoly firm is twice the decline in the perfectly competitive firm.

Use Figure 10-1 to answer questions 26 – 30:

FIGURE 10-1

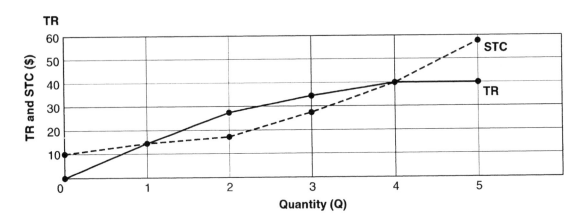

_____26. The total revenue (TR) curve indicates that:
    a. price (P) is constant regardless of output.
    b. total revenue increases at an increasing rate.
    c. marginal revenue (MR) is constant.
    d. P > MR.

_____27. Marginal revenue is zero:
    a. between outputs (Q) 4 and 5.
    b. only if Q = 0.
    c. at the break-even points, Q = 1 and Q = 4.
    d. when marginal cost is zero.

_____28. Total fixed cost (TFC) is:
    a. zero at the break-even points, Q = 1 and Q = 4.
    b. continuously declining as Q increases.
    c. $10 at every possible Q.
    d. Unable to calculate with the information provided.

____29. In the case shown above, profits are maximized:
    a. at the output (Q) with the maximum difference between short-run total cost (STC) and price.
    b. at the output (Q) at which STC is zero.
    c. at the output (Q) with the maximum positive difference between short-run total cost (STC) and total revenue (TR).
    d. at a level of output (Q) which is less than 1 and greater than 4.

____30. At the profit maximizing level of output, price (P) is:
    a. $28.
    b. equal to average revenue (AR) and equal to marginal revenue (MR).
    c. equal to average revenue (AR) which is $14.
    d. equal to marginal cost (MC) which is $3.

CHAPTER 11:

PRICE AND OUTPUT UNDER MONOPOLISTIC COMPETITION AND OLIGOPOLY

PART I: REVIEW OF CONCEPTS FROM PREVIOUS CHAPTER

Prior to reading chapter 11, match statements at left with the appropriate concept at right.

____1. Rule of profit maximization

____2. The long-run average cost decreases as production expands

____3. The additional cost associated with raising production

____4. If the firm's demand curve is horizontal the firm is a _____

____5. The monopolist's demand curve is _____ sloped

____6. The cross elasticity of demand is positive for such goods

____7. Total profits

____8. Long-run economic profits for a perfectly competitive firm

____9. They prevent potential competitors from entering the market

____10. Legal obstacles preventing potential competition

____11. It occurs when the price of a complementary good decreases

____12. A market with one seller

____13. Additional revenue generated from selling one more unit

____14. Charging different prices to different customers not based on cost differences

____15. Requiring customers who buy or lease one of the firm's products or services to buy or lease another of the firm's products or services when customers have different tastes but the monopolist cannot price discriminate

____16. International price discrimination

a. monopoly
b. price taker
c. rightward shift of demand curve
d. negatively
e. increasing returns to scale
f. barriers
g. legal barriers
h. substitute goods
i. marginal revenue
j. MR = MC
k. zero
l. marginal cost
m. (PQ – SAC*Q)
n. dumping
o. bundling
p. price discrimination

PART II: ANNOTATED CHAPTER OUTLINE

11. 1 MONOPOLISTIC COMPETITION: MANY SELLERS OF A DIFFERENTIATED PRODUCT

1. **Monopolistic competition**: where there are many sellers of a heterogeneous or differentiated product, and entry into or exit from the industry is rather easy in the long run

2. **Differentiated products**: products that are similar but not identical
3. **Product group**: lumping together all the sellers of a similar product

11.2 MONOPOLISTIC COMPETITION: SHORT-RUN AND LONG-RUN ANALYSIS

A. Price and Output Decisions Under Monopolistic Competition

1. The monopolistically competitive firm faces a highly price elastic demand curve, but which is negatively sloped; hence MR < P.
2. In the long run all monopolistically competitive firms break even and produce on the negatively sloped portion of their LAC curve
3. Excess capacity: the difference between the level of output indicated by the lowest point in the LAC curve and the monopolistic competitor's output when in long-run equilibrium

B. Product Variation and Selling Expenses

1. **Product variation**: changes in some of the characteristics of the product that a monopolistic competitor undertakes in order to make its products more appealing to consumers
2. **Selling expenses**: expenses that the firm incurs to advertise the product, increase its sales force, provide better service for their product, etc.

C. How Useful is the Theory of Monopolistic Competition? Criticisms include that it is difficult to define the market, in some markets product differentiation is slight, other markets have only a few firms, and impacts are only local

11.3 OLIGOPOLY: INTERDEPENDENCE AMONG THE FEW PRODUCERS IN THE INDUSTRY

1. **Oligopoly**: form of market organization in which there are few sellers of a homogeneous or differentiated product
2. **Duopoly**: only two sellers
3. **Pure oligopoly**: if the product is homogeneous
4. **Differentiated oligopoly**: if the product is differentiated
5. **Concentration ratio**: measurement of degree by which an industry is dominated by a few large firms

11.4 THE COURNOT AND THE KINKED-DEMAND CURVE MODELS

A. The Cournot Model: Interdependence Not Recognized

1. **Cournot model**: behavioral assumption that each firm, while trying to maximize profits, assumes that the other duopolist holds its output constant at the existing level
2. **Bertrand model**: behavioral assumption that each firm, while trying to maximize profits, assumes that the other duopolist holds its price constant at the existing level

B. The Kinked-demand Curve Model: Interdependence Recognized

1. **Kinked-demand curve model**: attempts to explain the price rigidity that is often observed in some oligopolistic markets

11.5   COLLUSION: CARTELS AND PRICE LEADERSHIP MODELS
1. **Collusion**: oligopolistic firms can avoid behavior that is detrimental to their general interests and adopt policies that increase their profits; can be overt or tacit
   A. **A Centralized Cartel Operates as a Monopolist**
      1. **Cartel**: formal organization of producers of a commodity
      2. **Centralized cartel**: sets the monopoly price for the commodity, allocates the monopoly output among the member firms, and determines how the monopoly profits are to be shared
   B. **Market Sharing Cartel**
      1. **Market sharing cartel**: member firms agree only on how to share the market
   C. **Price Leadership**
      1. **Price leadership**: firm generally recognized as the price leader starts the price change and the other firms in the industry quickly follow
      2. **Barometric firm**: the price leader who is not the dominant or largest firm

11.6   LONG-RUN ADJUSTMENTS AND EFFICIENCY IMPLICATIONS OF OLIGOPOLY
   A. **Long-Run Adjustments in Oligopoly**
      1. **Limit pricing**: artificial barrier to entry whereby existing firms charge a price low enough to discourage entry into the industry
   B. **Nonprice Competition Among Oligopolists**
      1. **Nonprice competition**: advertising, product differentiation and services
   C. **Welfare Effects of Oligopoly**: do not produce at lowest long-run average cost, can earn long-run profits, price is greater than the long-run marginal cost, advertising and product differentiation is beyond what is socially desirable

11.7   OTHER OLIGOPOLISTIC PRICING PRACTICES
   A. **Limit Pricing as a Barrier to Entry**: charging a price low enough to discourage entry into an industry
   B. **Cost-Plus Pricing: A Common Short-Cut Pricing Practice**
      1. **Cost-plus pricing**: firm estimates the average variable cost for a "normal" output level and then adds a certain percentage or markup over average variable cost to determine the price of the commodity
      2. **Markup**: set sufficiently high to cover average variable and fixed costs and also provide a profit margin for the firm

11.8   THE MARCH OF GLOBAL OLIGOPOLISTS: the trend toward formation of global oligopolies has accelerated due to internal growth and mergers, with the biggest growth in banking

---

⌘   AT THE FRONTIER   ⌘
THE ART OF DEVISING AIRFARES

The pricing of airline tickets illustrates most of the concepts presented in this chapter, as they are actually applied in a real-world oligopolistic market. The section shows the importance of market structure in output and pricing decisions, price leadership, price discrimination, the pricing of multiple products, and how they are all interrelated to marginal analysis in pricing as it is actually conducted in a major oligopolistic industry today.

PART III: KEY CONCEPTS IN THIS CHAPTER

1.   A monopolistically competitive industry is one where there are _____ sellers, each producing _____ or _____ products, and entry into or exit from the industry is rather _____ in the long run.
2.   Products that are similar but not identical are called _____ products. Lumping together all the sellers of a similar product is called a product _____.
3.   A monopolistically competitive firm is a price _____. Price _____ marginal revenue and the demand for the firm's product is **elastic/inelastic/somewhat elastic/perfectly elastic**.
4.   For a monopolistically competitive firm, the price _____ marginal cost of production at the profit-maximizing output level; hence, the criterion of _____ efficiency is violated.
5.   _____ is the difference between the level of output indicated by the lowest point on the LAC curve and the monopolistic competitor's output when in long-run equilibrium.
6.   The changes in some of the characteristics of the product that a monopolistic competitor undertakes in order to make its product more appealing to consumers are called _____.
7.   An industry with few sellers of a homogeneous or differentiated product is called a(n) _____. Such firms are price _____.
8.   The measurement of the degree by which an industry is dominated by a few large firms is the _____. The higher the percentage of total industry sales accounted for by the largest four or eight firms in the industry, the _____ the degree of competition within the industry.
9.   There **is one theory/are several theories** of the behavior of oligopoly firms. Among the key characteristics of oligopoly is that of **interdependence/independence**.
10.   The model that assumes that each firm, while trying to maximize profits, assumes the other duopolist holds its output constant at the existing level is the _____. If instead it was assumed that the other duopolist holds its price constant, then it would be the _____ model.
11.   The Cournot model **does/does not** recognize interdependence **contrary to/along with** the kinked-demand curve model.
12.   The _____ model attempts to explain the price rigidity that is often observed in some oligopolistic markets. This model's conclusions are that an oligopolistic firm

---

loses/gains revenues when it raises its price while the others do not follow, and **loses/gains** revenues when it decreases its price forcing a price war with other competitors.

13. Oligopolistic firms can avoid detrimental behaviors to their general interest, and thereby raise their profits, by engaging in _____. A formal organization of producers of a commodity is called a _____.

14. Setting the monopoly price for the commodity, allocating the monopoly output among the member firms, and determining how the monopoly profits are to be shared are functions of a(n) _____. If member firms agree only on how to share the market then it is called a(n) _____.

15. When a firm that is generally recognized as the price leader starts a price change, and the other firms in the industry quickly follow, it is called _____. The price leader who is not the dominant or largest firm is called a _____.

16. One artificial barrier to entry at the disposal of existing firms is that of charging a price low enough to discourage entry into the industry; this is called _____.

17. Oligopolists can compete on advertising, product differentiation, and service; this is called _____ competition.

18. The welfare effects of an oligopoly are that it **does/does not** produce at the lowest _____, **can/cannot** earn long-run profits, price is _____ than long-run marginal cost, advertising and product differentiation is **beyond/equal to** what is socially desirable.

19. The strategy of estimating the average variable cost for a "normal" output level and then adding a certain percentage or markup over the average variable cost to determine the price of the commodity is called _____ pricing.

20. The trend is towards the formation of _____. Such a phenomenon has accelerated due to **internal/external** growth and _____. The text mentions that the biggest growth is in _____.

PART IV: MULTIPLE-CHOICE QUESTIONS

___1. An industry with many sellers of a heterogeneous or differentiated product, and for which entry into or exit from it is rather easy in the long run is:
a. perfect competition.
b. monopoly.
c. oligopoly.
d. monopolistic competition.

___2. A monopolistic competitor is known to minimize long-run marginal cost (LMC) at output (Q) equal to 3 units, minimize long-run average cost (LAC) at Q = 6, and to be in equilibrium at Q = 48. How much excess capacity is present?
a. 1.2 units.
b. 3 units.
c. 1.8 units.
d. 4.8 units.

___3. The form of market organization in which there are few sellers of a homogeneous or differentiated product is:
   b. perfect competition.
   c. monopoly.
   d. oligopoly.
   e. monopolistic competition.

___4. The basic behavioral assumption of the Cournot model is that:
   a. supply creates its own demand.
   b. each firm, while trying to maximize profits, assumes the other duopolist holds its output constant.
   c. each firm, while trying to maximize profits, assumes the other duopolist increases output.
   d. each firm, while trying to maximize profits, assumes the other duopolist decreases output.

___5. The kinked-demand curve model attempts to explain:
   a. the behavior of firms in monopolistic competition.
   b. the price rigidity often observed in some oligopolistic models.
   c. price leadership among oligopolists.
   d. collusion among oligopolists.

___6. The purpose of a cartel is to:
   a. coordinate the policies of the member firms so as to increase profits.
   b. determine equilibrium.
   c. use the Cournot model to set policy
   d. use the kinked-demand curve model to set policy.

___7. When existing firms charge a price low enough to discourage entry into the industry, there is:
   a. a natural barrier into that industry.
   b. price leadership.
   c. limit pricing.
   d. cost-plus pricing.

___8. If the total market demand curve has a vertical axis intercept at $6, and if a potential entrant into the industry has a demand curve with a vertical axis intercept of $3, and if the potential entrant's long-run average total cost (LAC) curve is horizontal at $3 while the existing firm's LAC is horizontal at $1, then the:
   a. existing firm can sell all it wants at prices less than $1 and make a profit.
   b. potential entrant firm can sell all it wants at prices less than $3 and make a profit.
   c. potential entrant firm must absorb $2 (the difference between its LAC and that of the existing firm) as an extra cost of production to make a profit.
   d. existing firm can set price at $3 to discourage entry.

___9. Which sector of industry has grown the most during the past three decades?
   a. automobile
   b. airline
   c. banking
   d. textiles

___10. If the price of good X (Px) is $9, and if the average variable cost (AVC) of the good is $6, then the markup over AVC is:
   a. 30%.
   b. 50%.
   c. 33%.
   d. 67%.

___11. To avoid the possibility of starting a price war, oligopolists prefer to engage in:
   a. nonprice competition.
   b. cost-plus pricing.
   c. marginal cost pricing.
   d. regulated economic activity.

___12. If the largest firm in an oligopoly raises price (P) each production season and the other smaller firms quickly follow, then there must be:
   a. a price leader.
   b. a kinked-demand curve model which would explain this behavior.
   c. limit pricing.
   d. a Cournot model which would explain this behavior.

___13. The basic behavioral assumption followed in the kinked-demand curve model is that:
   a. price leadership determines the new price to set each production season.
   b. Limit pricing is the primary method for determining price.
   c. competitors will not follow price cuts but will follow price increases.
   d. competitors will follow price cuts but will not follow price increases.

___14. The degree by which an industry is dominated by a few large firms is measured by:
   a. the income elasticity of demand.
   b. the price elasticity of demand.
   c. concentration ratios.
   d. the marginal rate of technical substitution.

___15. If the minimum long-run average cost (LAC) for a firm is $5 at output (Q) equal to 10 units, then added product variation and selling expenses will result in the LAC curve shifting:
   a. down and the minimum LAC will be at an output greater than 10.
   b. up and the minimum LAC will be at an output less than 10.
   c. down and the minimum LAC will be at an output less than 10.
   d. up and the minimum LAC will be at an output equal to 10.

____16. For a given market demand, as short-run profits appear in an average or representative firm in monopolistic competition, the:
    a. supply curve shifts right until it is tangent to a long-run marginal cost (LMC) curve.
    b. demand curve shifts left until it is tangent to a long-run average cost (LAC) curve.
    c. demand curve shifts right until it is tangent to a long-run average cost (LAC) curve.
    d. supply curve shifts left until it is tangent to a long-run marginal cost (LMC) curve.

____17. The lumping together of all the sellers of similar products is called:
    a. a product group.
    b. heterogeneous oligopoly.
    c. homogeneous oligopoly.
    d. monopolistic competition.

____18. The changing of some of the characteristics of a product in order to make it more appealing to consumers is:
    a. product variation.
    b. product grouping.
    c. advertising.
    d. reducing excess capacity.

____19. The Vincent Company has incurred expenses of $10,000 to increase its sales force and to better service their product. The expenses are called:
    a. advertising expenses.
    b. selling expenses.
    c. assets and liabilities.
    d. costs of goods sold.

____20. One reason the theory of monopolistic competition has fallen out of favor is:
    a. product groups explained everything important about monopolistic competition.
    b. product differentiation is too varied within a product group to be explained.
    c. in markets with strong brand preferences, the theory of oligopoly better explains the behavior of firms.
    d. that it has failed to explain the behavior of firms located closely to one another.

____21. In a local retail market, all the dry cleaning companies provide services in a:
    a. differentiated oligopoly market structure.
    b. pure oligopoly market structure.
    c. monopolistic competition market structure.
    d. duopoly market structure.

___22. Concentration ratios for 8-firm groups are:
    a. the same for all industries.
    b. equal to 4-firm groups in the same industry.
    c. less than 4-firm groups in the same industry.
    d. greater than 4-firm groups in the same industry.

___23. The Cournot model is considered to be unrealistic because:
    a. moves and counter-moves are not adequately addressed.
    b. interdependence is not recognized in each step of the model.
    c. only behavior of duopolists can be explained.
    d. it has too many simplifying assumptions.

___24. A serious criticism of the kinked-demand curve model is:
    a. competitors never follow a price decrease by a firm in this type of industry.
    b. competitors never fail to follow a price increase by a firm in this type of industry.
    c. the model can rationalize rigid prices but not explain why the price at the kink occurs.
    d. prices change more often than once a season.

___25. Collusion in setting price and dividing markets is most likely to occur in:
    a. monopoly with a unique product.
    b. perfect competition with the production of a heterogeneous good.
    c. monopolistic competition with a product group.
    d. centralized oligopoly in the form of a cartel.

Use Figure 11-1 to answer questions 26 – 30:

FIGURE 11-1

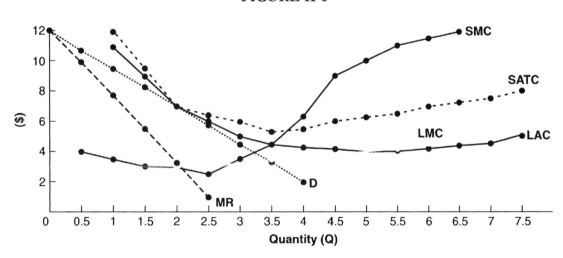

___26. The model represents a:
    a. differentiated or heterogeneous oligopoly in short-run equilibrium.
    b. pure or homogeneous oligopoly in long-run equilibrium.

    c. perfectly competitive firm with profits of zero, since price (P) equals $7.50 which equals short-run average total cost (SATC).

    d. monopolistically competitive firm in long-run equilibrium.

____27. The overall most efficient level of long-run output (Q) is:

    a. 5 units since long-run marginal cost (LMC) equals long-run average cost (LAC) of $4.

    b. 2 units since marginal revenue (MR) equals short-run marginal cost (SMC) of $2.90.

    c. 2 units since P = SAC of $9.

    d. 4 units since the SAC curve is minimum at $5.83.

____28. The best long-run level of output (Q) is:

    a. 5 units since long-run marginal cost (LMC) equals long-run average cost (LAC) of $4.

    b. 2 units since marginal revenue (MR) equals short-run marginal cost (SMC) of $2.90 and profit is zero.

    c. 4 units since the SAC curve is minimum at $5.83.

    d. Cannot be determined from the information provided.

____29. If a perfectly competitive firm were to have its long-run average cost curve (LAC) superimposed in this figure, then long-run equilibrium would be at:

    a. the same level of output as the equilibrium shown.

    b. 5 units, where a downward sloping demand curve would intersect minimum LAC.

    c. 5 units, where a horizontal demand curve would be tangent to minimum LAC.

    d. 2.5 units, where SMC has a minimum of $2.50.

____30. If long-run equilibrium is achieved, then the:

    a. short-run equilibrium could not be as shown since profits are equal to zero.

    b. short-run equilibrium is as shown with profits equal to zero.

    c. firm shown must be making an accounting profit of zero.

    d. firm shown is making an accounting loss.

CHAPTER 12:

GAME THEORY AND OLIGOPOLISTIC BEHAVIOR

PART I: REVIEW OF CONCEPTS FROM PREVIOUS CHAPTER

Prior to reading chapter 12, match statements at left with the appropriate concept at right.

____1. Additional revenue generated from selling one more unit
____2. Percentage change in quantity supplied divided by percentage change in price
____3. Goods with negative cross elasticity of demand
____4. An organization that transforms inputs into outputs
____5. Labor, capital, land and entrepreneurship
____6. Sellers or buyers whose actions cannot affect the market price
____7. Charging different prices to different customers not based on cost differences
____8. Additional output decreases as more variable inputs are added
____9. Change in output divided by change in input
____10. Products that are similar but not identical
____11. Lumping together all the sellers of a similar product
____12. Only two sellers in an industry
____13. Market organization where there are few sellers of a homogeneous or differentiated product
____14. Measurement of the degree by which an industry is dominated by a few large firms
____15. The price leader which is not the dominant or largest firm

a. inputs
b. price takers
c. firm
d. elasticity of supply
e. law of diminishing marginal returns
f. marginal revenue
g. marginal product
h. price discrimination
i. complements
j. oligopoly
k. differentiated products
l. concentration ratios
m. product group
n. duopoly
o. barometric firm

PART II: ANNOTATED CHAPTER OUTLINE

12.1 GAME THEORY: DEFINITION, OBJECTIVES, AND USEFULNESS

1. **Game theory**: choice of an optimal strategy in conflict situations
2. **Players**: decision makers whose behavior we are trying to explain and predict
3. **Strategies**: potential choices to change price, to develop new or differentiated products, to introduce a new or different advertising campaign, to build excess capacity, and all other such actions that affect the sales and profitability of the firm and its rivals

4. **Payoff**: outcome or consequence of each strategy
5. **Payoff matrix**: table giving the payoffs from all the strategies open to the firm and the rivals' responses
6. **Zero-sum game**: one in which the gain of one player comes at the expense and is exactly equal to the loss of the other player
7. **Nonzero-sum game**: one in which the gains or losses of one player do not come at the expense of or provide equal benefit to the other

12.2   DOMINANT STRATEGY AND NASH EQUILIBRIUM
1. **Dominant strategy**: optimal choice for a player no matter what the opponent does
2. **Nash equilibrium**: situation where each player chooses an optimal strategy, given the strategy chosen by the other player

12.3   THE PRISONER'S DILEMMA, PRICE AND NONPRICE COMPETITION, AND CARTEL CHEATING
A. **The Prisoner's Dilemma: Definition and Importance**
1. **Prisoner's dilemma**: situation where each firm adopts its dominant strategy but each could do better by cooperating
B. **Price and Nonprice Competition, Cartel Cheating and the Prisoner's Dilemma**: all can be analyzed using the same type of payoff matrix

12.4   REPEATED GAMES AND TIT-FOR-TAT STRATEGY
1. **Repeated games**: many-move games
2. **Tit-for-tat**: do to your opponent what he or she has just done to you

12.5   STRATEGIC MOVES
A. **Threats, Commitments, and Credibility**
1. **Strategic move**: one that influences the other person's choice in a manner favorable to one's self, by affecting the other person's expectations of how one's self would behave
B. **Entry Deterrence**: deter market entry by threatening to lower price and impose loss on a potential entrant

12.6   STRATEGIC MOVES AND INTERNATIONAL COMPETITIVENESS: game theory can be used to analyze strategic trade and industrial policies a nation can use to gain a competitive advantage over other nations

12.7   STRATEGIC BEHAVIOR WITH RISK: most real-world business decisions are made in the fact of risk or uncertainty, with the firm not knowing the exact payoff or outcome of the strategic moves open to it, and this greatly complicates the development and conduct of business strategy by the firm

---

⌘ AT THE FRONTIER ⌘
THE VIRTUAL CORPORATION

The virtual corporation is a temporary network of independent companies coming together with each contributing its core technology to quickly take advantage of fast-changing opportunities.

PART III: KEY CONCEPTS IN THIS CHAPTER

1. The choice of an optimal strategy in conflict situations is called _____ theory.

2. The decision makers whose behavior we are trying to explain and predict are the _____.

3. The potential choices to change price, to develop new or differentiated products, to introduce a new or different advertising campaign, and to build excess capacity are called _____; the intentions of such actions are to affect the _____ and _____ of the firm and its rivals.

4. A game usually consists of players, rules, _____, and _____.

5. The _____ is the table that gives the payoffs from all the strategies open to the firm and its rivals.

6. The _____ is the optimal choice for a player no matter what the opponent does, whereas the _____ is the situation where each player chooses his or her optimal strategy, given the strategy chosen by the other player.

7. The _____ is the situation where each firm adopts its dominant strategy but each could do better by cooperating.

8. A _____ game is one in which the players are allowed to make binding agreements.

9. The prisoner's dilemma games have a(n) _____ strategy equilibrium since the best strategy for each player is independent from that of the other players, and the outcome is the same for each player.

10. Many-move games are called _____ games, whereas the "do to your opponent what he or she has done to you" games are called _____ games.

11. In repeated games, the _____ strategy occurs when one player punishes the other for cheating on an agreement, but then returns to the agreement once the violator learns his/her lesson.

12. The strategy that influences the other person's choice in a manner favorable to one's self, by affecting the other person's expectations of how one's self would behave is called a(n) _____.

13. Threatening to lower price and impose loss on a potential entrant is a strategy of _____.

14. On the international scene, the objective of a nation's strategic moves and industrial policies is to gain a _____ over other nations.

15. Nonprice competition and the incentive to cheat on a cartel can be studied by the _____.

---

16. One of the problems in applying the analysis of strategic moves to government industrial and trade policies is the difficulty in accurately forecasting the _____ of such policies.
17. A good tool to analyze the scenarios of price and nonprice competition, the cartel cheating and the prisoner's dilemma is the _____.
18. The Cournot model of duopoly is an example of _____.
19. In a case of the prisoner's dilemma, suspects in a crime will have combined years of imprisonment minimized if one **confesses/does not confess** to the crime while the other **confesses/does not confess**.
20. The first number in a cell within the payoff matrix refers to **profits/sales/the payoff of one player** while the second number refers to **losses/expenses/the payoff of the second player**.

PART IV: MULTIPLE-CHOICE QUESTIONS

___1. Game theory is concerned with:
   a. the choice of an optimal strategy in conflict situations.
   b. transitivity of indifference orderings.
   c. transitivity of preference orderings.
   d. how to calculate the odds of winning.

___2. The dominant strategy is the:
   a. optimal strategy for a player in the majority of the possible outcomes.
   b. one which gets the consumer to purchase a good.
   c. optimal choice for a player no matter what the opponent does.
   d. one which is impossible for both players to achieve simultaneously.

___3. When each player can do better by cooperating rather than by each adopting his or her dominant strategy, they are in:
   a. Nash equilibrium.
   b. a tit-for-tat strategy.
   c. prisoner's dilemma.
   d. repeated games strategy.

___4. "Do to your opponent what he or she has just done to you," is a summarization of the:
   a. prisoner's dilemma.
   b. Nash equilibrium.
   c. Pareto optimum solution
   d. tit-for-tat strategy.

___5. "There must be a commitment that the firm making the threat is ready to carry it out for the threat to be credible" a fundamental to what T. Schelling called a:
   a. prisoner's dilemma.
   b. Nash equilibrium.
   c. Pareto optimum solution
   d. strategic move.

___6. One of the serious shortcomings of using strategic moves to analyze government industrial and trade policies is:
   a. that the governments do not cooperate.
   b. that trade should be free of any governmental policies.
   c. the difficulty in accurately forecasting the outcome of such policies.
   d. zero sum games.

___7. The strategy of entry deterrence is usually the result of:
   a. threatening to lower price which would impose a loss on the potential entrant.
   b. threatening to raise price which would impose a loss on the potential entrant.
   c. advertising.
   d. product development.

___8. For the tit-for-tat strategy to work:
   a. it requires a reasonably stable set of players.
   b. there must be a large number of players.
   c. each firm must ignore other firms that cheat.
   d. the game should not be repeated.

___9. Nonprice competition and the incentive to cheat can be studied by:
   a. long-run economies and diseconomies of scale.
   b. the prisoner's dilemma.
   c. a constrained Nash equilibrium.
   d. a non-constrained dominant strategy.

___10. Only when each player has chosen his or her optimal strategy given the strategy of the other player is there:
   a. a prisoner's dilemma.
   b. the tit-for-tat strategy.
   c. repeated game strategy.
   d. Nash equilibrium.

___11. The decision makers in game theory are called:
   a. players.
   b. consumers.
   c. producers.
   d. resource owners.

___12. The table with the results from all strategies to the firm and the rivals' responses is
the:
   a. demand schedule.
   b. Edgeworth box.
   c. payoff matrix.
   d. contingency table.

___13. The potential choices of players to change price or develop new or differentiated
products are called:
   a. the payoff matrixes.
   b. strategies.
   c. constrained optimization.
   d. minimax decisions.

___14. The outcome or consequence of a strategy is called a(n):
   a. payoff.
   b. payoff matrix.
   c. equilibrium.
   d. disequilibrium.

___15. The analogy of game theory to military strategy includes:
   a. destroying the competition.
   b. the chain of command.
   c. being aggressive with an element of surprise.
   d. filtering information from the top down.

___16. In a two-by-two matrix used by duopolists, there are _____ possible outcomes.
   a. 2
   b. any number of
   c. 8
   d. 4

___17. The first number in a cell within a payoff matrix refers to _____ and the second
number to _____.
   a. profits, losses
   b. sales, expenses
   c. the payoff of one player, the payoff of the other player
   d. revenues, expenses

___18. A payoff matrix reveals that firm A has a dominant strategy to engage in product
promotion regardless of whether firm B does or does not do the same. Which one
of the following is true?
   a. It is possible for firm B to have a dominant strategy at the same time.
   b. It is impossible for firm B to have a dominant strategy at the same time.
   c. It is impossible to have a Nash equilibrium when firm B reacts second.
   d. One must use repeated game strategy to determine the effect on firm B.

___19. How many numbers must one change in a payoff matrix, which illustrates a dominant strategy for each duopolist, to show a Nash equilibrium?
    a. All numbers in each cell must be changed.
    b. Only one number in a single cell must be changed.
    c. Both numbers in a single cell must be changed.
    d. All the numbers associated with one of the duopolists must be changed.

___20. The Cournot model of duopoly is an example of:
    a. Nash equilibrium.
    b. a dominant strategy for both duopolists.
    c. prisoner's dilemma.
    d. a tit-for-tat model.

___21. In a case of prisoner's dilemma, what is the only way (by acting in their own self interest) that suspects in a crime will have combined years of imprisonment minimized?
    a. Collusion between the suspects so that both do not confess.
    b. One confesses to the crime, but the other does not confess.
    c. Both suspects must confess.
    d. Each suspect adopts his/her own dominant strategy.

___22. By banning cigarette advertising on television, the legislation had the unintended effect of:
    a. decreasing the profits of cigarette producers.
    b. increasing the cost of production for cigarette producers.
    c. solving the prisoner's dilemma for cigarette producers.
    d. imposing a Nash equilibrium on cigarette producers.

___23. In the example of airline price wars in 1992, all domestic airlines:
    a. earned profits by cutting prices.
    b. immediately followed price increases but not price decreases.
    c. earned an all-time high revenue per passenger mile.
    d. could have benefited in the long-run by adopting American Airline's new fare structure.

___24. In single-move prisoner's dilemma games:
    a. tit-for-tat behavior is revealed.
    b. cooperation is not likely to be achieved.
    c. cooperation is likely to be achieved.
    d. there is always Nash equilibrium.

___25. Computer simulations have revealed that tit-for-tat behavior is the best strategy for:
    a. Nash equilibrium.
    b. simultaneous dominant strategies.
    c. repeated prisoner's dilemma games.
    d. any strategic move.

Use the information below to answer questions 26 – 30:
The following table reveals the profits in millions of dollars that members of a cartel will make under the conditions of cheating or not cheating on a collusive agreement among members.

TABLE 12-1

Firm A ?   Firm B ?

	Cheat	Not Cheat
Cheat	3,3	6,2
Not Cheat	2,6	4,4

___26. It is in the self-interest of firm B to:
  a. not cheat on the agreement even if firm A cheats.
  b. not cheat on the agreement if firm A does not cheat.
  c. reveal to the other members of the cartel what firm A will do.
  d. cheat regardless of what firm A does.

___27. It is in the self-interest of firm A to:
  a. cheat on the agreement regardless of what firm B does.
  b. reveal to the other members of the cartel what firm B will do.
  c. not cheat on the agreement if firm B does not cheat.
  d. not cheat on the agreement even if firm B cheats.

___28. When both firms operate in their own self-interest, the solution is the cell that shows the profits of:
  a. 3,3.
  b. 6,2.
  c. 2,6.
  d. 4,4.

___29. Why will the cells showing profits of 6,2 and 2,6 not be stable solutions?
  a. Because the sum of the numbers in each cell is 8.
  b. Because the absolute difference of the numbers in each cell is 4.
  c. Neither firm can rely on the other not to cheat.
  d. Cell 3,3 is better.

___30. How can the cell showing profits of 4,4 be reached?
  a. Firm A would not tell firm B what it will do in advance.
  b. Firm B would not tell firm A what it will do in advance.
  c. Both firms agree to not agree on strategy.
  d. Both firms agree on strategy.

CHAPTER 13:

MARKET STRUCTURE, EFFICIENCY, AND REGULATION

Prior to reading chapter 13, match statements at left with the appropriate concept at right.

___1. Wants exceed the limited supply
___2. Quantity supplied falls short of the quantity demanded
___3. Occurs when the indifference curve is everywhere
    flatter than the budget line
___4. Demand curve for this inferior good is positively
    sloped since the income effect dominates the
    substitution effect
___5. Normal good with income elasticity between 0 and 1
___6. Total product divided by the quantity of labor used
___7. Total obligations of the firm per time period for all
    the variable inputs
___8. The most efficient plant results from the best output
    level at the lowest possible cost
___9. Charging different prices to various customers without
    cost justification
___10. Reflects the interdependence between duopolists
___11. Situation where each firm adopts its dominant strategy
    but each could do better by cooperating
___12. Do to your opponent what he/she has done to you
___13. Outcome of a strategy
___14. Many-move games
___15. Rule of profit maximization

a. tit-for-tat
b. Giffen good
c. scarcity
d. corner solution
e. shortage
f. necessity
g. prison's dilemma
h. TVC
i. AP_L
j. long-run equilibrium
k. payoff
l. Cournot equilibrium
m. price discrimination
n. MR = MC
o. repeated games

PART II: ANNOTATED CHAPTER OUTLINE

13.1 MARKET STRUCTURE AND EFFICIENCY

1. **Efficiency**: the best level of output for a firm under any form of market organization is that at which marginal revenue equals marginal cost. However, unlike perfect competition (where P = MR) at the best level of output in imperfect competition the marginal benefit to consumers from the

last unit of the commodity consumed exceeds the marginal cost that the firm incurs to produce it

13.2 MEASURING MONOPOLY POWER
 A. The Lerner Index as a Measure of Monopoly Power
  1. **Lerner Index:** ratio of the difference between price and marginal cost to price. The index can have a value between zero and one; the closer the value is to one the greater the degree of monopoly power
 B. Concentration and Monopoly Power: The Herfindahl Index
  1. **Herfindahl index:** sum of the squared values of the market sales shares of all the firms in the industry. In general, the greater the value of the index the greater the degree of monopoly power in the industry
  2. The Justice Department's guidelines for mergers use the Herfindahl index as an indicator of the effect of the merger on concentration in the industry
 C. Contestable Markets: Effective Competition Even With Few Firms
  1. **Theory of contestable markets:** even if an industry has a single firm or only a few firms it would still operate as if it were perfectly competitive if entry is "absolutely free" and if exit is "entirely costless"

13.3 SOCIAL COSTS AND DYNAMIC BENEFITS OF MONOPOLY POWER
Perfect competition cannot be the model for dynamic efficiency, but neither can powerful monopolies and tightly knit cartels. What is needed for technical progress is a blend of the two

13.4 CONTROLLING MONOPOLY POWER: ANTITRUST POLICY
  1. **Sherman Antitrust Act:** conspiracy in restraint of trade or commerce is illegal
  2. **Conscious parallelism:** adoption of similar policies by oligopolists in view of their recognized interdependence
  3. **Clayton Act:** prohibits mergers which substantially lessen competition

13.5 PUBLIC-UTILITY REGULATION
 A. Public Utilities as Natural Monopolies: natural monopoly refers to the case in which a single firm can supply the entire market more efficiently than a number of firms could. In industries like local electrical, gas, and water to have more than one such firm in a given market would lead to duplication of supply lines and higher costs per unit
 B. Difficulties in Public-Utility Regulation
  1. **Averch-Johnson or AJ effect:** overinvestment or underinvestment in plant and equipment resulting from the wrong public-utility rates being set

13.6 THE DEREGULATION MOVEMENT
  1. **Deregulation movement:** since the 1970's in the United States, we have seen the deregulation of many industries including air travel, trucking, railroads, banking and telecommunications. The general purpose of deregulation is to increase competition and efficiency in the affected industries

13.7 REGULATING INTERNATIONAL COMPETITION: VOLUNTARY EXPORT RESTRAINTS

    1. **Voluntary export restraints (VER)**: where an important country induces another nation to reduce its exports of a commodity "voluntarily," under the threat of higher all-around trade restrictions, when these exports threaten an entire domestic industry

13.8 SOME APPLICATIONS OF MARKET STRUCTURE, EFFICIENCY, AND REGULATION

    A. Regulating Monopoly Price: set price equal to short-run average total cost or to short-run marginal cost

    B. Regulation and Peak-Load Pricing

        1. **Peak-load pricing**: charge the lower price equal to the higher marginal cost in peak periods

    C. Regulation and Transfer Pricing

        1. **Transfer pricing**: need to determine the price of intermediate products sold by one semi-autonomous division of a large-scale enterprise and purchased by another semi-autonomous division of the same enterprise

---

⌘ AT THE FRONTIER ⌘
FUNCTIONING OF MARKETS AND EXPERIMENTAL ECONOMICS

Experimental economics is the new field of economics that seeks to understand how real world markets actually work by conducting laboratory experiments assuming different institutional settings and levels of information.

PART III: KEY CONCEPTS IN THIS CHAPTER

1.   _____ is reached when the marginal revenue equals the _____.
2.   The sum of the squared values of the market shares of all the firms in the industry is the _____.
3.   The theory that stipulates that even if an industry has a single firm or only a few firms, it would still operate as if it were perfectly competitive if entry is "absolutely free" and exit is "entirely costless" is that of _____.
4.   The ratio of the difference between price and marginal cost to price is the _____.
5.   According to the text, a fast-growing field is that of _____ economics.
6.   The first antitrust law was the **Morrell/Sherman** Act of **1862/1890**.
7.   The Sherman Act made **legal/illegal** any conspiracy in restraint of _____ or _____.
8.   _____ is the adoption of similar policies by oligopolists in view of their recognized interdependence.
9.   The Clayton Act made illegal _____ which substantially lessen competition.

10. If a firm completely monopolizes an industry, the Herfindahl index would have a value of _____.

11. By squaring the market share of each firm, the Herfindahl index gives much more weight to **larger/smaller** firms in the industry.

12. When a single firm can supply the entire market more efficiently than a number of firms could it is a _____. The most commonly cited example that the text discusses is that of _____.

13. The overinvestment or underinvestment in plant and equipment resulting from the wrong public-utility rates being set is the _____ effect.

14. The phenomenon of _____ is when an importing country induces another nation to reduce its exports of a commodity "voluntarily," under the threat of higher all-around trade restrictions, when these exports threaten an entire domestic industry.

15. Regulating the monopoly price is setting the price equal to _____ or _____.

16. Peak-load pricing is charging the _____ price equal to the _____ marginal cost in peak periods.

17. _____ describes the need to determine the price of intermediate products sold by one semi-autonomous division of a large-scale enterprise and purchased by another semi-autonomous division of the same enterprise.

18. If a firm is a natural monopolist, its marginal cost will probably be **above/below** the firm's SAC curve even at large quantities of output; thus, if the firm is required by regulatory agencies to charge a price equal to the MC, it would incur a _____.

19. If the regulatory agency imposes the average cost pricing method on a firm, it would force the firm to earn _____ economic profits.

20. According to the text, the _____ in the United States was characterized by a movement toward _____ of industries.

PART IV: MULTIPLE-CHOICE QUESTIONS

___1. The marginal revenue (MR) equals $50 and the marginal cost (MC) equals $35 at output (Q) 25 for a monopoly firm. The MC curve has a positive slope. The firm should:
   a. increase Q until MC = MR = $50.
   b. increase Q until MC = MR = $35.
   c. increase Q until MC = MR.
   d. decrease Q until MC = MR.

___2. For a perfectly competitive firm, the Lerner index is equal to:
   a. zero since price (P) equals marginal cost (MC).
   b. zero since price elasticity of demand (?) is zero.
   c. infinity since ? is infinity.
   d. Cannot be calculated without knowledge of marginal revenue (MR).

___3. In imperfectly competitive markets:
   a. the marginal benefit (MB) to consumers from the last unit exceeds the marginal cost (MC) that the firm incurs in producing it.
   b. the MB to consumers from the last unit is less than the MC that the firm incurs in producing it.
   c. the MB to consumers from the last unit equals the MC that the firm incurs in producing it.
   d. price (P) is less than MC.

___4. What did the Sherman Antitrust Act make illegal?
   a. monopoly
   b. price (P) greater than marginal cost (MC)
   c. price (P) less than marginal cost (MC)
   d. formal or informal agreements or arrangements.

___5. When a single firm can supply a service to the entire market more efficiently than a number of firms could, there is a:
   a. cartel.
   b. monopolistic competition.
   c. duopoly.
   d. natural monopoly.

___6. Since the 1970s in the United States:
   a. a growing deregulation movement has resulted in deregulation of air travel, trucking, railroads, banking, and telecommunications.
   b. a growing regulation movement has resulted in regulation of air travel, trucking, railroads, banking, and telecommunications.
   c. savings and loan associations have proven to be the best example of the advantages of deregulation.
   d. deregulation has resulted in more profitable airlines.

___7. When an importing country induces another nation to reduce its exports of a good without force, there is voluntary:
   a. export restraints.
   b. import restraints.
   c. trade restraints.
   d. exchange expansion.

___8. If the government was to regulate a monopoly with a price ceiling (below the equilibrium price), then the resulting:
   a. demand (D) curve would have a vertical section.
   b. Marginal revenue (MR) curve would be continuous without a gap.
   c. D curve would have a horizontal section.
   d. MR curve would not equal price (P) at all prices on the D curve.

___9. When intermediate products are sold by one semi-autonomous division of a large-scale enterprise and purchased by another semi-autonomous division of the same enterprise, there is:
   a. limit pricing.
   b. transfer pricing.
   c. marginal cost pricing.
   d. full cost pricing.

___10. When voluntary export restraints are successful:
   a. monopoly profits are captured by the importing country.
   b. they have all the economic effects of an equivalent import tariff.
   c. they eliminate jobs in the importing country.
   d. they eliminate jobs in the exporting country.

___11. The general purpose of deregulation is to:
   a. standardize the product or service deregulated.
   b. discourage competition.
   c. raise the price of the deregulated good or service.
   d. increase competition and efficiency.

___12. Overinvestment or underinvestment in plant and equipment resulting from the wrong public-utility rates being set is known as the _____ effect.
   a. Clayton Act
   b. Sherman Antitrust Act
   c. substitution
   d. Averch-Johnson

___13. The Clayton Act prohibits:
   a. mergers that substantially lessen competition.
   b. monopoly.
   c. conspiracy to monopolize.
   d. conscious parallelism.

___14. Measuring the social costs of imperfect competition by comparing it to perfect competition:
   a. results in negative social costs.
   b. results in social costs equal to zero.
   c. may not be correct since the need for large-scale production may not be possible in perfect competition.
   d. cannot be correct since the firm in perfect competition faces a downward sloping demand curve.

___15. When economists test theories to determine how markets actually work in the real world, they are using:
   a. normative economics.
   b. experimental economics.
   c. deductive reasoning.
   d. contestable-market theory.

___16. When entry into a market is absolutely free and exit is entirely costless, the theory of contestable markets:
   a. holds that monopoly profits will be earned.
   b. gives a price (P) greater than minimum long-run average cost (LAC).
   c. contends that a monopolist will behave as a perfect competitor with a horizontal demand curve.
   d. contends that a monopolist will behave as a perfect competitor with a downward sloping demand curve.

___17. The Herfindahl index is:
   a. lower with more monopoly power in an industry.
   b. higher with less monopoly power in an industry.
   c. used to measure the monopoly power of a particular firm in an industry.
   d. equal to 10,000 when there is a single firm in the industry.

___18. If the Lerner index equals zero, then price elasticity of demand (?) is:
   a. infinity, indicating a perfectly competitive firm.
   b. infinity, indicating a single-firm industry.
   c. a positive fraction between 0 and 1.
   d. equal to 1.

___19. When oligopolists adopt similar policies in view of their recognized interdependence, there is:
   a. conscious parallelism, which the courts have ruled to be legal.
   b. conscious parallelism, which the courts have ruled to be illegal.
   c. collusion.
   d. the A-J effect.

___20. If a manager in a regulated public utility is granted a salary higher than what he or she would be paid in his or her next best alternative employment, then:
   a. salaries in the private sector must rise.
   b. there are regulation inefficiencies.
   c. social costs are zero.
   d. the A-J effect must hold.

___21. Why is there a regulatory lag when setting utility rates?
   a. Time must be allowed for the forces of supply and demand to work.
   b. Competitors demand that the utility not have a comparative advantage.
   c. Public hearings must be considered before regulatory commissions can set rates.
   d. There must be a lag because the regulatory commissions are part of the government.

___22. With peak-load pricing:
   a. the same price is charged all the time.
   b. a low price is charged when demand is high.
   c. a low price is charged when costs are high.
   d. a high price is charged when demand is high.

____23. In the model explaining transfer pricing:
   a. individual demand curves are summed horizontally.
   b. the marginal cost (MC) curves of various firm divisions are added vertically.
   c. individual demand curves are summed vertically.
   d. the marginal cost (MC) curves of various firm divisions are added horizontally.

____24. To guarantee that a regulated monopoly would earn economic profits of zero, the regulatory commission would set price (P):
   a. equal to marginal cost (MC).
   b. equal to long-run average cost (LAC).
   c. at a ceiling above minimum LAC.
   d. at a floor below minimum LAC.

____25. Compared to a single price policy with two consumers, peak-load pricing results in:
   a. both prices above the original single price.
   b. both prices below the original single price.
   c. a net loss in consumer welfare.
   d. a net gain in consumer welfare.

Use Figure 13-1 to answer questions 26 – 30:

FIGURE 13-1

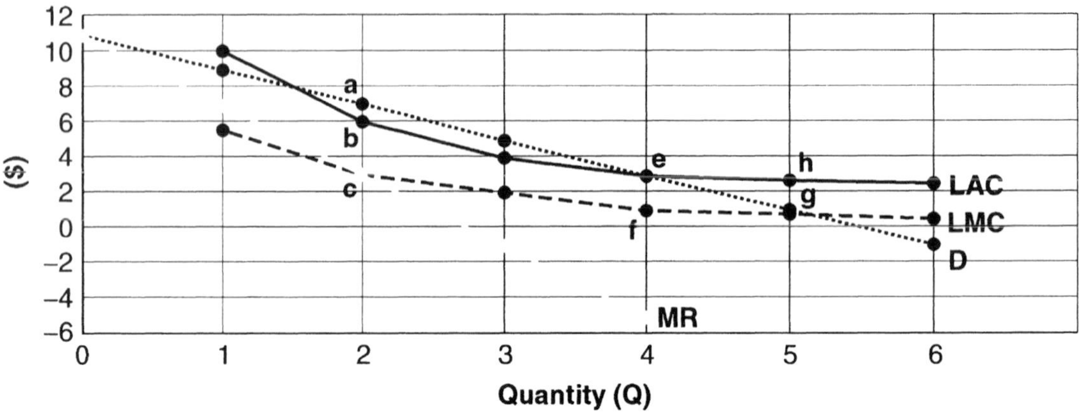

____26. The shape of the long-run average cost (LAC) curve indicates:
   a. perfect competition.
   b. monopolistic competition.
   c. natural monopoly.
   d. oligopoly.

___27. If a regulatory commission set price (P) at $3, corresponding to point e on the demand curve, then the public utility will:
   a. break even in the long run.
   b. need a subsidy to stay in business.
   c. make a profit in the long run.
   d. break up into smaller firms.

___28. If a regulatory commission set P as in the preceding question, then consumer welfare will:
   a. not be affected.
   b. increase by the area ehg.
   c. decrease by the area efg.
   d. decrease by the area fehg.

___29. If a regulatory commission set P at $1, corresponding to point g on the demand curve, then the public utility will:
   a. make a per-unit profit equal to the distance ef.
   b. have a per-unit loss equal to the distance hg.
   c. gain consumer welfare equal to the area fehg.
   d. lose consumer welfare equal to the area fegh.

___30. If this utility were completely unregulated, then P would be set:
   a. at point e on the demand curve.
   b. at point g on the demand curve.
   c. at point a on the demand curve.
   d. somewhere between point a and point g on the demand curve.

CHAPTER 14:

INPUT PRICE AND EMPLOYMENT UNDER PERFECT COMPETITION

Prior to reading chapter 14, match statements at left with the appropriate concept at right.

____1. Satisfaction from consuming goods
____2. Land, labor, capital, and entrepreneurship
____3. If preferences of people change, consumption rises
____4. Assuming other things remain constant
____5. No tendency to move away from this situation
____6. Additional cost associated with raising production
____7. Measure of responsiveness of consumers to price changes
____8. A market with only one seller
____9. Total profits
____10. They prevent firms from entering an industry
____11. Law which states that the marginal product of workers decreases as more workers are hired
____12. They show various combinations of two inputs that can be used to produce a specific level of output
____13. Case where output changes are proportional to the changes in inputs
____14. Cartel where member firms agree only on how to share the market
____15. Shows the amount of a commodity that a consumer would purchase per unit of time at various income levels, while holding prices and tastes constant

a. equilibrium
b. marginal cost
c. ceteris paribus
d. inputs
e. monopoly
f. utility
g. (P - SAC)*Q
h. elasticity of demand
i. change in demand
j. constant returns to scale
k. barriers
l. market-sharing cartel
m. law of diminishing returns
n. isoquants
o. Engel curve

PART II: ANNOTATED CHAPTER OUTLINE

14.1 PROFIT MAXIMIZATION AND OPTIMAL INPUT EMPLOYMENT

To maximize profits, the firm must use the optimal or least-cost input combination to produce the best level of output. Thus the profit-maximizing rule is that the firm should hire all inputs until the marginal product of each input times the marginal revenue or price of the commodity is equal to the price of each input

14.2 THE DEMAND CURVE OF A FIRM FOR AN INPUT
A. The Demand Curve of a Firm for One Variable Input
1. **Derived demand**: the demand for an input is derived from the demand for the final commodities that the input is used to produce
2. **Marginal revenue product (MRP)**: extra income given by the marginal product (MP) of the input times the marginal revenue (MR)
3. **Value of the marginal product (VMP)**: when the firm is a perfect competitor in the product market, its marginal revenue is equal to the commodity price and the marginal revenue product (MRP) is called the value of marginal product (VMP)
4. **Marginal expenditure (ME)**: extra costs from hiring an additional unit of input
B. The Demand Curve of a Firm for One of Several Variable Inputs
1. **Complementary inputs**: when both labor and capital are variable they are complements; thus when the firm hires more labor it will also employ more capital

14.3 THE MARKET DEMAND CURVE FOR AN INPUT AND ITS ELASTICITY
A. The Market Demand Curve for an Input: derived from the individual firms' demand curves for the input, but it is not simply the horizontal summation of those demands; the effect of changes in commodity prices on the MRP curves must be considered
B. Determinants of the Price Elasticity of Demand for an Input
1. The price elasticity of demand for an input is defined as the percentage change in the quantity demanded of the input resulting from a given percentage change in its price
2. The determinants of the price elasticity of demand for an input are: the number of substitutes for the input, the demand for the final good produced using the input, the elasticity of supply for substitute inputs, and the percentage of the total cost spent on the input

14.4 THE SUPPLY CURVE OF AN INPUT
A. The Supply of Labor by an Individual
1. **Intermediate good**: a good used in the production of another good
B. Substitution and Income Effects of a Wage Increase: used to determine the total effects of a wage change, the two effects work in opposite directions for a backward-bending supply curve
C. The Market Supply Curve for an Input: horizontal summation of the supply curves of individual suppliers of the input

14.5 PRICING AND EMPLOYMENT OF AN INPUT
1. **Marginal productivity theory**: theory of input pricing and employment that states that the price of an input equals its marginal revenue product (MRP)

14.6   **INPUT PRICE EQUALIZATION AMONG INDUSTRIES, REGIONS, AND COUNTRIES**

   A. **Input Price Equalization Among Industries and Regions of a Country**: if labor is mobile, the supply of labor will shift towards regions with higher wages and away from regions with lower wages

   B. **Input Price Equalization Among Countries**: if labor is not mobile, wage rates can be equalized through international trade

14.7   **ECONOMIC RENT: AN UNNECESSARY PAYMENT TO BRING FORTH THE SUPPLY OF AN INPUT**

   1. **Economic rent**: portion of the payment to the supplier of any input (not just land) that is in excess of the minimum amount necessary to retain the input in its present use

   2. **Quasi rent**: payment made to temporarily fixed inputs

14.8   **ANALYSIS OF LABOR MARKETS UNDER PERFECT COMPETITION**

   A. **Substitution and Income Effects of a Wage Rate Change**: as the wage rises the individual substitutes work for leisure and the individual demands more of normal goods including leisure

   B. **Overtime Pay and the Supply of Labor Services**

   1. **Overtime pay**: hourly wage increases after a specific number of hours worked per day

   C. **Wage Differentials**

   1. **Compensating wage differentials**: wage differences that compensate workers for the nonmonetary differences among jobs

   2. **Noncompeting groups**: occupations requiring different capacities, skills, education, and training, and therefore, receiving different wages

   D. **Effect of Minimum Wages**

   1. **Unemployment gap**: difference between the quantity supplied of labor and the quantity demanded of labor at the above-equilibrium wage

   2. **Disemployment effect**: firms employ fewer workers at the above-equilibrium wage

---

⌘   AT THE FRONTIER   ⌘
DO MINIMUM WAGES REALLY REDUCE EMPLOYMENT?

Minimum wages lead to a disemployment effect and to an even greater unemployment gap.

PART III: KEY CONCEPTS IN THIS CHAPTER

1.   The demand for an input is _____ from the demand for the final commodities that the input is used to produce.

2.   The marginal revenue product (MRP) is the extra _____ given by the _____ of the input times the _____.

Use the following information to answer questions 3 – 5: When the firm has 9 workers it produces 81 units of output each day and sells that output for $891. When the firm has 10 workers it produces 88 units of output each day and has revenues of $968.

3.	The marginal product (MP) of the 10th worker is _____ units of output per day while the marginal revenue product (MRP) of the 10th worker is _____.

4.	The price of the firm's product is _____ per unit when the firm sells 81 units and is _____ when the firm sells 88 units. The firm **is/is not** a price maker in the commodity market, so it faces a _____ demand curve for its output.

5.	The marginal revenue for the firm is _____ since the price **equals/exceeds** the marginal revenue from selling another unit of the commodity.

6.	The value of the marginal product (VMP) is the _____ times the marginal product (MP) of the input. In a perfectly competitive output market, the VMP **equals/exceeds** the marginal revenue product (MRP).

7.	The marginal expenditure (ME) is the _____ cost from hiring an additional unit of a(n) _____. Mathematically, ME = ? _____/ ? _____.

Use the following information to answer questions 8 and 9: When a firm has 9 workers its total labor costs are $450 per day. If it hires a 10th worker, its labor cost goes up to $500 per day.

8.	The marginal expenditure (ME) of labor is _____ per day and **decreases/increases/remains the same** as the firm hires additional workers; thus, the firm is an input price _____.

9.	The firm faces a _____ labor **supply/demand** curve. The daily wage rate equals _____ per worker.

10.	Based on the firm's demand for its product and its cost of production, the firm will keep on hiring additional workers as long as the marginal revenue product (MRP) is _____ than the marginal expenditure (ME). The firm maximizes its profits by hiring the quantity of inputs where MRP _____ ME.

11.	The marginal revenue product (MRP) curves slope _____ as the firm hires **more/fewer** units of an input because the law of _____ marginal product sets in.

12.	When the firm hires more labor, it will also employ more capital; thus, the two inputs are _____.

13.	When the firm buys more capital, it reduces the number of workers it employs; in this case the two inputs are _____.

14.	The determinants of the price elasticity of demand for an input are the number of _____ for the input, the _____ for the final good using the input, the elasticity of _____ for substitute inputs, and the percentage of total _____ spent on the input.

15.	The effects of a wage increase can be decomposed into the _____ effect and the _____ effect; the directions of the two effects are _____ for a backward-bending supply of labor curve.

16.	A theory of input price and employment that the text mentions is the _____ theory.

17. If labor is _____, then the supply of labor will shift towards regions with higher wages and away from regions with lower wages. This explains the input price _____ among industries and regions of a country or among countries.

18. The portion of the payment to the supplier of any input that is in excess of the minimum amount necessary to retain the input in its present use is called a(n) _____.

19. Occupations requiring different capacities, skills, education, and training, and which therefore receive different wages, are called _____.

20. The possible effects of minimum wages that the text describes are the creation of a(n) _____ at above-equilibrium wages and those of _____.

PART IV: MULTIPLE-CHOICE QUESTIONS

___1. The least-cost combination of inputs (labor, L, and capital, K) is given by:
    a. setting the marginal product of labor (MP_L) equal to the marginal product of capital (MP_K).
    b. setting the MP_L per dollar spent on labor equal to the MP_K per dollar spent on capital.
    c. the combination of inputs which maximizes output (Q).
    d. the combination of inputs with lowest prices.

___2. The demand for any input used to produce a final good or service is a _____ demand.
    a. derived
    b. consumer
    c. kinked
    d. relative

___3. The market demand for labor is the:
    a. horizontal summation of individual firms' demand curves for labor.
    b. vertical summation of individual firms' demand curves for labor.
    c. horizontal summation of individual firms' demand curves for labor after the effect on the final good's price is factored into the calculation.
    d. vertical summation of individual firms' demand curves for labor after the effect on the final good's price is factored into the calculation.

___4. When deriving the supply curve for labor (S_L):
    a. the absolute values of the slopes of the budget lines give the wage rates (w).
    b. the budget line is shifted parallel to itself.
    c. w and the price of capital (r) are changed simultaneously.
    d. budget lines cannot be used since this uses isocost lines.

___5. The theory of input pricing and employment is called:
    a. supply and demand theory.
    b. indifference curve analysis.
    c. isoquant-isocost analysis.
    d. marginal productivity theory.

___6. If the price of labor in region 1 (w₁) is $25 and the price of labor in region 2 (w₂) is $50 and the demand for labor is identical in both regions, if labor can move between the two regions, then:
   a. the supply of labor in region 1 will increase.
   b. the supply of labor in region 2 will decrease.
   c. the supply of labor in region 1 will decrease and the supply of labor in region 2 will increase.
   d. the supply of labor in region 1 will increase and the supply of labor in region 2 will decrease.

___7. If the equilibrium price of labor (w) is $35 and quantity of labor (L) is 250, and if the straight-line supply curve for labor has a vertical axis intercept of $15, then the economic rent is:
   a. 250($35) = $8,750.
   b. 250($35 - $15) = $5,000.
   c. 250($35 - $15)(0.5) = $2,500.
   d. $8,750 - $2,500 = $6,250.

___8. The substitution effect due to a wage increase causes an individual to work_____ and the income effect causes the individual to work _____.
   a. less, more
   b. more, less
   c. less, less
   d. more, more

___9. If the equilibrium price of labor (w) is $3.90 at a quantity of labor (L) of 5 million workers, then a minimum wage placed on this market would be placed:
   a. above w = $3.90 and result in an excess supply of labor, *ceteris paribus*.
   b. above w = $3.90 and result in an excess demand for labor, *ceteris paribus*.
   c. below w = $3.90 and result in an excess supply of labor, *ceteris paribus*.
   d. below w = $3.90 and result in an excess demand for labor, *ceteris paribus*.

___10. Any payment made to temporarily fixed inputs is called a(n):
   a. rent.
   b. economic rent.
   c. quasi rent.
   d. wage or interest payment, depending on the type of input.

____11. If in country 1 there is an excess demand for labor at wage rate w_1 equal to $22, and if in country 2 there is an excess supply for labor at wage rate w_2 equal $28, and if the supply of labor is identical in both countries, if labor cannot migrate between the two countries, then:
   a. the wage in country 1 would fall if the demand for labor decreases.
   b. the wage in country 2 would rise if the demand for labor decreases.
   c. the wage in country 1 would rise if the demand for labor decreases and the wage in country 2 would fall if the demand for labor increases.
   d. the wage in country 1 would rise if the demand for labor decreases and the wage in country 2 would fall if the demand for labor decreases.

____12. If at a quantity of labor of 200 units firms are willing to pay a wage (w) of $30 per unit of labor but individuals must have $50 to supply 200 units, then:
   a. the equilibrium quantity of labor is more than 200 units.
   b. at w = $50 there is an excess supply of labor.
   c. at w = $30 there is an excess supply of labor.
   d. the equilibrium w is greater than $50 or less than $30.

____13. The market supply curve for labor is:
   a. the horizontal summation of individual suppliers' supply curves for labor.
   b. the vertical summation of individual suppliers' supply curves for labor.
   c. the horizontal summation of individual suppliers' supply curves for labor after the effect on the final good's price is factored into the calculation.
   d. the vertical summation of individual suppliers' supply curves for labor after the effect on the final good's price is factored into the calculation.

____14. The price elasticity of demand for an input is lower:
   a. the larger the price elasticity of demand for the commodity which uses the input.
   b. the greater the number of available substitutes for the input.
   c. the smaller the percentage of total cost spent on the input.
   d. the longer the period of time allowed for the adjustment to the change in the input price.

____15. For a firm that operates as a perfect competitor in the product market, the marginal product of labor (MRP_L) is:
   a. the marginal product of labor (MP_L) divided by the price of labor (w).
   b. $(MP_L)(P) = VMP_L$, where P is the price of the final product and VMP_L is the value of the marginal product of labor.
   c. $(MP_L)(MR)$ if the P > MR.
   d. less than the VMP_L.

____16. The marginal cost (MC) of the firm to produce an additional unit of output (Q) is:
   a. MP_L/w where MP_L is the marginal product of labor and w is the wage rate.
   b. w/MP_L.
   c. (w)(L) where L is the quantity of labor.
   d. w.

___17. The extra cost of hiring an input is:
  a. marginal revenue product (MRP).
  b. MRP/w.
  c. VMP is P > MR.
  d. marginal expenditure (ME).

___18. If three coordinates of wage and quantity of labor are given as ($2, 5), ($2.50, 7) and ($3, 6), then:
  a. the budget line has shifted either out or in parallel to itself.
  b. both the price of labor (w) and the price of capital (r) have changed.
  c. there is a backward-bending supply curve of labor.
  d. there is a backward-bending demand curve for labor ($D_L = MRP_L$).

___19. What has prevented real manufacturing wages in the leading industrial countries from converging as much as predicted by the theory?
  a. the gap in wages in the different countries
  b. transportation cost, trade restrictions, and other market imperfections
  c. supply and demand
  d. cheap foreign labor

___20. If the supply of an input (such as land) is completely fixed, then the supply curve for that input has:
  a. a slope of infinity.
  b. an elasticity of infinity.
  c. a positive slope.
  d. a negative slope.

___21. When the overtime wage is greater than the standard time wage:
  a. a change in the shape of the indifference curve map explains an increase in work hours.
  b. there is a parallel shift in the budget line.
  c. the slope of the budget line becomes steeper with rotation around a point along that line but not at either intercept.
  d. the slope of the budget line becomes steeper with rotation around a point along the horizontal axis intercept of that line.

___22. When a wage is paid for a carpenter working at a super-fund pollution cleanup site is greater than that paid to a carpenter using the same skills but working to construct a home, there are:
  a. compensating wage differentials.
  b. noncompeting groups.
  c. perfect labor markets.
  d. discrimination.

____23. When a minimum wage distorts a labor market and firms employ fewer workers at the above-equilibrium wage, the reduction in employment is called:
   a. a shortage of labor.
   b. a total unemployment gap.
   c. the disemployment effect.
   d. the excess supply of labor.

____24. Occupations requiring different capacities, skills, education and training:
   a. have wages which can be accounted for by compensating wage differentials.
   b. are noncompeting groups and are likely to receive different wages.
   c. should be paid the same wage for the same number of hours worked.
   d. are in the same labor market.

____25. A change in the wage results in:
   a. an income effect.
   b. a substitution effect.
   c. both an income and a substitution effect.
   d. neither an income nor a substitution effect.

Use Figure 14-1 to answer questions 26 – 30:

FIGURE 14-1

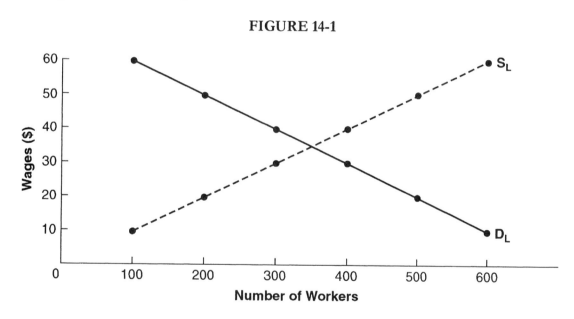

____26. If the number of workers were fixed at 200, then:
   a. the market would clear at a wage (w) of $35.
   b. the gap between what firms are willing to pay and what individuals will accept is $50.
   c. the gap between what firms are willing to pay and what individuals will accept is $20.
   d. the gap between what firms are willing to pay and what individuals will accept is $30.

___27. What is the highest wage (w) which firms are willing to pay regardless of the supply of labor?
   a. $35
   b. $60
   c. $10
   d. $50

___28. What is the lowest wage (w) which individuals are willing to accept regardless of the demand for labor?
   a. $35
   b. $60
   c. $10
   d. $50

___29 If a minimum wage were placed at $50 by government regulation, then the disemployment effect:
   a. is the excess supply of labor 500 – 200 = 300 units.
   b. is 500 – 350 = 150 units due to an increase in the quantity supplied of labor.
   c. is 350 – 200 = 150 units due to a decrease in the quantity demanded of labor.
   d. is not present.

___30. What would happen if a minimum wage were placed at $20 by government regulation?
   a. The disemployment effect is a shortage of labor given by 500 – 200 = 300 units.
   b. The disemployment effect is 500 – 350 = 150 units due to an increase in the quantity demanded of labor.
   c. The disemployment effect is 350 – 200 = 150 units due to a decrease in the quantity supplied of labor.
   d. Nothing, since a minimum wage has no effect when placed below the equilibrium wage.

INPUT PRICE AND EMPLOYMENT UNDER IMPERFECT COMPETITION

PART I: REVIEW OF CONCEPTS FROM PREVIOUS CHAPTER

Prior to reading chapter 15, match statements at left with the appropriate concept at right.

___1. Wage differences that result from nonmonetary differences between jobs

___2. When quantity demanded is unresponsive to price hikes

___3. Measure of responsiveness of quantity demanded to changes in income

___4. Theory of "MRP equals the wage rate"

___5. When firms earn below normal profits they _____.

___6. In a competitive output market the MRP equals _____.

___7. Normal profits are also called _____.

___8. A change in the wage rate will cause cost curves to _____.

___9. Additional output per additional unit of an input purchased

___10. Total revenues minus total explicit and implicit costs

___11. Demand for inputs depends on demand for outputs

___12. Result of a wage rate below equilibrium

___13. The extra costs associated with hiring additional units of inputs

___14. The extra revenue associated with hiring additional units of inputs

___15. As more variable inputs are hired, the slope of the marginal product curve tends to decrease

a. exit
b. zero economic profits
c. VMP
d. MRP
e. law of diminishing returns
f. marginal product
g. derived demand
h. shortage of labor
i. compensating wage differentials
j. marginal productivity theory
k. shift
l. economic profits
m. income elasticity
n. inelastic demand
o. ME

PART II: ANNOTATED CHAPTER OUTLINE

15.1 PROFIT MAXIMIZATION AND OPTIMAL INPUT EMPLOYMENT

To maximize profits, the firm must use the optimal or least-cost input combination to produce the best level of output. Thus the profit-maximizing rule is that the firm should hire all inputs until the marginal product of each input times the marginal revenue of the commodity is equal to the price of each input. (NOTE: unlike the case in perfect competition, price and marginal revenue are no longer equal!)

15.2 THE DEMAND CURVE OF A FIRM FOR AN INPUT
A. The Demand Curve of a Firm for One Variable Input
1. **Marginal revenue product (MRP)**: extra revenue earned by an imperfect competitor from hiring an additional unit of the input; given by the marginal product (MP) of the input times the marginal revenue (MR)
2. **Monopolistic exploitation**: the excess of the value of marginal product of labor (VMP_L) over the marginal revenue product of labor (MRP_L) at the point where $MRP_L = w$

B. The Demand Curve of a Firm for One of Several Variable Inputs
The demand curve is derived from two positions of the marginal revenue product (MRP). On the first there is movement along the curve as the wage decreases, and on the second there is a shift to the right due to decreased utilization of substitutes for labor.

15.3 THE MARKET DEMAND CURVE, AND INPUT PRICE AND EMPLOYMENT
If firms using the input are monopolists, the market demand curve for the input is the horizontal summation of the individual firms' demand curves. If the firms using the input are oligopolists or monopolistic competitors in the final goods market, the market demand curve for the input is derived the same way as when the firms are perfect competitors.

15.4 MONOPSONY: A SINGLE FIRM HIRING AN INPUT
1. **Monopsony**: a single firm hiring an input
2. **Marginal expenditure (ME)**: the extra cost of hiring an additional unit of an input
3. **Marginal expenditure on labor (ME_L)**: extra cost of hiring an additional unit of labor
4. **Marginal expenditure on capital (ME_K)**: extra cost of hiring an additional unit of capital
5. **Oligopsony**: the case when there are only a few firms hiring a homogeneous or differentiated input
6. **Monopsonistic competition**: the case where there are many firms hiring a differentiated input

15.5 MONOPSONY PRICING AND EMPLOYMENT OF ONE VARIABLE INPUT
1. **Monopsonistic exploitation**: excess of marginal revenue product (MRP) of the input over the input price; the monopsonist hires until the MRP equals the ME, and the ME is greater than the price of the input

15.6 MONOPSONY PRICING AND EMPLOYMENT OF SEVERAL VARIABLE INPUTS
Marginal cost equals marginal revenue equals the marginal expenditure on labor divided by the marginal product of labor equals the marginal expenditure on capital divided by the marginal product of capital

15.7 INTERNATIONAL MIGRATION AND THE BRAIN DRAIN

1. **Brain drain**: the emigration of skilled workers and professionals

15.8 ANALYSIS OF IMPERFECT INPUT MARKETS

A. **Regulation of Monopsony**: set a minimum price for an input where marginal revenue product intersects the supply curve for the input; causes the monopsonist to behave as a perfect competitor in the input market and eliminates monopsonistic exploitation

B. **Bilateral Monopoly: A Monopsonistic Buyer Facing a Monopolistic Seller**
   1. **Bilateral monopoly**: when the single buyer of a product or input faces the single seller of the product or input; price and output are determined by the relative bargaining strength of the two.

C. **Effect of Labor Unions on Wages**
   1. **Labor union**: an organization of workers that seeks to increase the wages and the general welfare of union workers through collective bargaining with employers

D. **Economics of Discrimination in Employment**
   1. **Discrimination in employment**: can take many forms, but the text discusses that between male and female workers of equal productivity.

⌘ AT THE FRONTIER ⌘
DISCRIMINATION, AND GENDER AND WAGE DIFFERENTIALS

Data shows differences in earnings of different categories of workers (i.e., female/male, black/white). Empirical studies seem to indicate the most of the differences are due to differences in productivity (based on different levels of education, training, etc.); whether and to what extent the remaining difference is due to discrimination or to other productivity factors has yet to be settled. To overcome possible discrimination, the **comparable-worth** doctrine proposes the evaluation of jobs (in terms of the knowledge and skills required, etc.) and the enforcement of equal pay for comparable jobs.

PART III: KEY CONCEPTS IN THIS CHAPTER

1. The optimal input employment decision that maximizes the firm's profits is that of the _____ which equals the _____ , which equals the price of _____ divided by the _____ of labor which equals the rental price of _____ divided by the _____ of capital.

2. The _____ is the extra revenue earned by an imperfect competitor from hiring an additional unit of an input.

3. The excess of the VMP_L over the MRP_L is called _____.

4. The demand curve of a firm for one of several variable inputs is derived from two positions of the _____ curve. On the first there is _____ the curve

as the wage decreases, and on the second there is a _____ to the
_____ due to decreased utilization of _____ for labor.

5. The market demand curve for an input by monopolists is the _____ of the individual firms' demand curves.

6. If the firms using the input are oligopolists or monopolistic competitors in the output market, the market demand curve for an input is derived **similarly to/differently from** the situation of _____ firms.

7. A single firm hiring an input is a(n) _____.

8. An increase in the wage rate means that _____ workers will be employed, _____. A 6% increase in the wage rate will cause the total worker income to _____ when the number of hired workers falls by less than 6%, meaning that the labor demand is _____.

9. The _____ substitutes there are for labor the more elastic the demand for labor.

10. The case of only a few firms hiring a homogeneous or differentiated input is that of a(n) _____, whereas the case of many firms hiring a differentiated input is that of a(n) _____.

11. The excess of marginal revenue product of the variable input over the input price is _____.

12. The employment decision of several variable inputs based on a monopsony price strategy is based on the _____ which equals the _____, which equals _____ of labor divided by the _____ of labor which equals the _____ of capital divided by the _____ of capital.

13. The phenomenon of emigration of skilled workers and professionals is called the _____.

14. Regulation of monopsony is to set a minimum price for an input where the _____ intersects the _____ curve for the input.

15. The situation of a monopsonistic buyer facing a monopolistic seller is that of a(n) _____ monopoly.

16. The organization of workers that seeks to increase the wages and the general welfare of those workers through collective bargaining with employers is a(n) _____ . Leaders of such organizations tend to _____ immigration by foreigners into the United States.

17. Suppose the demand for non-unionized workers is elastic whereas that of unionized workers is inelastic. A 10% increase in the wage rate will cause a larger loss of jobs for **unionized/non-unionized** workers. Therefore it should be a major long-term goal of union leaders to **lower/raise** the elasticity of demand for union labor.

18. A labor union can try to increase the wages of its members by _____ the supply of union labor that employers must hire, bargaining for a wage that is _____ equilibrium, or _____ the demand for union labor.

19. When the demand for the firm's product becomes more elastic, the demand for the labor that produces that product becomes **more/less** elastic.

20. The phenomenon of differences in average salary and/or in employment between males and females of equal productivity is called _____.

PART IV: MULTIPLE-CHOICE QUESTIONS

____1. For profit maximization, marginal revenue (MR) equals:
   a. the marginal product of labor (MP_L) divided by the price of labor (w).
   b. $(MP_L)(w)$.
   c. w/ MP_L.
   d. $w - MP_L$.

____2. If the marginal revenue product of labor (MRP_L) is $50 and the marginal revenue (MR) is $5, then:
   a. marginal product of labor (MP_L) is 10.
   b. VMP_L is $10.
   c. marginal expenditure for labor (ME_L) is 10.
   d. marginal cost (MC) is 10.

____3. When the final good is produced in an oligopolistic industry as opposed to being produced by a monopoly firm:
   a. the market demand curve for an input is the horizontal summation of individual firms' demand curves for the input when it's an oligopoly but the vertical summation of the curves when it's a monopoly.
   b. the market demand curve for an input is the vertical summation of individual firms' demand curves for the input when it's an oligopoly but the horizontal summation of the curves when it's a monopoly.
   c. the price (P) decline for the final good causes an upward shift in each firm's demand curve for labor in oligopoly but not in monopoly.
   d. the price (P) decline for the final good causes a downward shift in each firm's demand curve for labor in oligopoly but not in monopoly.

____4. When a single firm hires an input there is a _____ which faces a(n) _____ market supply of the input.
   a. monopoly, upward sloped
   b. monopsony, upward sloped
   c. monopoly, horizontal
   d. monopsony, horizontal

____5. At profit maximization, if the marginal expenditure (ME) is $75 and the marginal product of labor (MP_L) is $25, then:
   a. marginal revenue (MR) is $3.
   b. MR = $5.
   c. MR = $15.
   d. MR = $0.33.

____6. For profit maximization in monopoly pricing when employing more than one variable input, marginal cost (MC) is equal to the:
   a. marginal product of labor (MP_L) divided by the marginal expenditure on labor (ME_L).
   b. MP_K/ME_K where K is capital.

    c. ME_L/MP_L where L is labor.

    d. $ME_K - MP_K$ where K is capital.

___7. The net gain from immigration for a nation can be measured by:

    a.   the area under a marginal revenue product of labor (MRP_L) curve up to a specific level of labor (L).

    b.   the wage (w_1) times L_1.

    c. $(w_1)(L_1)$ minus $(w_2)(L_2)$ where the subscript 2 is associated with values after immigration.

    d.   the area formed under the MRP_L curve after $(w_1)(L_1)$ minus $(w_2)(L_2)$.

___8. When there is regulation of a monopsonist by setting the wage (w) at $30, the new:

    a.   supply curve for labor has a kink in it at $30.

    b.   marginal revenue product of labor (MRP_L) curve has a kink in it at $30.

    c.   supply curve for labor is discontinuous at $30.

    d.   marginal revenue product of labor (MRP_L) curve is discontinuous at $30.

___9. When analyzing the impact of gender discrimination in employment for a specific job, one must make a:

    a.   horizontal summation of the male supply (S_m) and the female supply (S_f) curves.

    b.   vertical summation of the male supply (S_m) and the female supply (S_f) curves.

    c.   horizontal summation of the male marginal cost curve (MC_m) and the female marginal cost curve (MC_f).

    d.   vertical summation of the male marginal cost curve (MC_m) and the female marginal cost curve (MC_f).

___10. A union can increase wages (w) by:

    a.   decreasing the demand for labor (L).

    b.   decreasing the supply of L.

    c.   making sure there is excess demand for L at wages below the equilibrium w.

    d.   increasing the supply of L.

___11. One of the two bilateral monopoly equilibrium solutions is given by a monopolist's:

    a.   marginal revenue product (MRP) intersecting a monopsonist's marginal cost (MC).

    b.   marginal revenue product (MRP) intersecting a monopsonist's marginal expenditure (ME).

    c.   marginal revenue (MR) intersecting the same monopolist's MC curve.

    d.   demand curve intersecting the same monopolist's supply curve.

___12. By setting a minimum price for labor at the point where the marginal revenue product of labor (MRP_L) intersects the market supply curve of labor, the monopsonist can be made to behave as a(n):

    a.   imperfect competitor with the elimination of monopsonistic exploitation.

    b.   perfect competitor with the elimination of monopsonistic exploitation.

    c.   perfect competitor without the elimination of monopsonistic exploitation.

    d.   imperfect competitor without the elimination of monopsonistic exploitation.

____13. The immigration laws of the United States and other industrial countries:
   a. favor unskilled labor, except for migrants.
   b. favor unskilled labor, including migrants.
   c. discriminate against professional people.
   d. favor skilled labor and professional people.

____14. In the case of profit maximization in monopsony pricing when employing more than one variable input, if marginal cost (MC) is $25 and the marginal product of labor (MP_L) is 10, then the marginal revenue product of labor (MRP_L) is:
   a. $2.50.
   b. $2500.
   c. $250.
   d. $25.

____15. When the marginal expenditure on labor (ME_L) is greater than the price of labor (w), there is:
   a. a perfectly competitive input market.
   b. monopsonistic exploitation.
   c. bilateral monopoly.
   d. monopoly power.

____16. Oligopsony refers to the case of a few firms which:
   a. produce a homogeneous product.
   b. hire a homogeneous or differentiated input.
   c. produce a differentiated product.
   d. both produce a homogeneous product and hire a homogeneous input.

____17. If the supply curve of labor (S_L) has a positive slope, then the marginal expenditure on labor (ME_L) curve:
   a. will lie above S_L.
   b. will lie below S_L.
   c. is the S_L.
   d. has a negative slope.

____18. When the supply or demand for an input changes, then:
   a. the resulting new equilibrium does not occur instantaneously.
   b. the resulting new equilibrium must occur instantaneously.
   c. the impact on the equilibrium for a final good which uses the input must occur instantaneously.
   d. neither the supply curve nor the demand curve for the final good which uses the input will shift.

____19. The demand curve of a firm for one of several variable inputs is given by:
   a. at least two points on at least two marginal expenditure (ME) curves.
   b. one point on ME_1 and one point on ME_2.
   c. at least two points on a single marginal revenue product (MRP) curve.
   d. one point on MRP_1 and one point on MRP_2.

___20. Joan Robinson called the excess of the value of marginal product of labor (VMP_L) of labor over the marginal revenue product of labor (MRP_L):
   a. monopoly power.
   b. market power.
   c. the waste from monopolistic power.
   d. monopolistic exploitation.

___21. If the price of capital (r) is $30 and the marginal revenue (MR) is $1.50, then the marginal product of capital (MP_K) is:
   a. 0.05.
   b. 0.5.
   c. 20.
   d. $31.50.

___22. When the marginal revenue product (MRP) for an input is known to be $25 and the marginal expenditure (ME) on the same input is $32, the firm should:
   a. hire more of this input in order to maximize profits.
   b. hire less of this input in order to maximize profits.
   c. switch to the exclusive use of an input for which ME = MRP.
   d. do nothing, *ceteris paribus*.

___23. If all firms using an input are monopolists in their respective product markets, then the market demand for the input is the horizontal summation of the individual firms':
   a. demand curves for the input.
   b. demand curves for the input which have shifted due to the change in the price of the input.
   c. marginal expenditure (ME) curves for that input.
   d. ME curves for that input which have shifted due to the change in the price of the input.

___24. The extra cost incurred to hire each additional worker is called marginal:
   a. cost.
   b. revenue.
   c. expenditure.
   d. revenue product.

___25. Monopsonistic competition refers to the case where there are:
   a. many sellers of differentiated products.
   b. many buyers of differentiated inputs.
   c. few sellers of differentiated products.
   d. few buyers of differentiated inputs.

Use Figure 15-1 to answer questions 26 – 30:

FIGURE 15-1

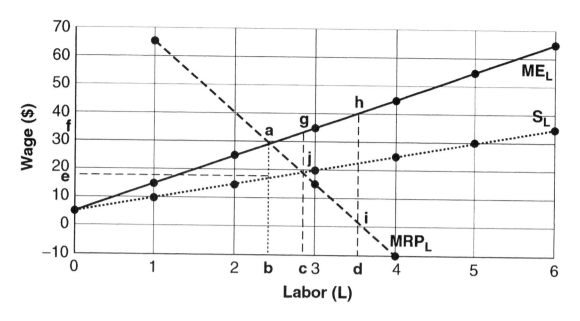

Labor (L)

____26. Without regulation, the monopsonist would be in equilibrium at:
a. point j, where the supply of labor (S_L) is equal to the marginal revenue product of labor (MRP_L).
b. point j, where the supply of labor (S_L) is equal to the marginal revenue product of labor (MRP_L) and the wage (w) is indicated by point g.
c. point a, where the marginal expenditure on labor (ME_L) is equal to the MRP_L and w is at point f.
d. point a, where the ME_L is equal to the MRP_L and w is at point e.

____27. Monopolistic exploitation can be shown by the distance between points:
a. h and i.
b. f and e.
c. g and j.
d. Cannot be determined from the information provided.

____28. If starting at point b, the monopsonist increased the use of labor (L) to the quantity at point d, then:
a. even more units of labor should be used to maximize profits.
b. fewer units of labor should be used since $MRP_L > ME_L$ at point d.
c. nothing should change since profits are maximized.
d. the monopsonist's total profit would fall by (h – i)L.

___29. If the wage (w) were set at $20, then the supply curve of labor (S_L) would:
   a. remain unchanged.
   b. be horizontal until point j then follow the upward sloping S_L.
   c. be horizontal at $20 regardless of the amount of L used.
   d. have a discontinuous section.

___30. If the wage (w) were set at $20, then the marginal expenditure on labor (ME_L) curve would:
   a. remain unchanged.
   b. be horizontal at $20 regardless of the amount of L used.
   c. have a discontinuous section.
   d. have a kink at point j.

CHAPTER 16:

FINANCIAL MICROECONOMICS: INTEREST, INVESTMENT, AND THE COST OF CAPITAL

Prior to reading chapter 16, match statements at left with the appropriate concept at right.

____1. Abstract representation of the real world

____2. Highest benefits foregone when a choice is made

____3. Consumption of such a good rises when income falls

____4. Everything else held constant

____5. Economics of individual behavior

____6. Change in consumption caused by a change in price

____7. When price of X rises, demand for Y shifts to the right; X and Y must be _____.

____8. Horizontal demand curve

____9. (STC – TFC)/Q

____10. Long-run unit costs decline as output rises

____11. Profit-maximizing rule from the input side

____12. In a perfectly competitive output market, this and the MRP are equal

____13. Q/L

____14. The single buyer of a product or input faces the single seller of the product or input

____15. A single firm hiring an input

a. law of demand

b. MRP = ME

c. *ceteris paribus*

d. opportunity cost

e. AVC

f. MP_L

g. theory

h. VMP

i. substitutes

j. economies of scale

k. inferior good

l. microeconomics

m. perfectly elastic

n. monopsony

o. bilateral monopoly

PART II: ANNOTATED CHAPTER OUTLINE

16.1 LENDING-BORROWING EQUILIBRIUM

A. Lending

1. **Endowment position:** a combination of income (or goods) received this period and next period

2. **Rate of interest (r):** premium received by an individual next year by lending money today

B. Borrowing

1. **Wealth:** individual's income or endowment this year plus the present value of next year's income or endowment

C. **The Market Rate of Interest with Borrowing and Lending**

The equilibrium rate of interest is determined where the demand curve for borrowing intersects the supply curve for lending.

16.2 SAVING-INVESTMENT EQUILIBRIUM

A. **Saving-Investment Equilibrium without Borrowing and Lending**
1. **Production possibilities curve**: shows how much a company can produce and consume next year by saving part of this year's output and investing it to increase next year's output
2. **Saving**: act of refraining from present consumption
3. **Investment**: formation of new capital assets

B. **Saving-Investment Equilibrium with Borrowing and Lending**
1. **Market line**: its slope shows the rate at which the individual can borrow or lend in the market

C. **The Market Rate of Interest with Saving and Investment, Borrowing and Lending**
1. The equilibrium rate of interest is determined where the demand curve for investment intersects the supply curve for savings.

16.3 INVESTMENT DECISIONS

1. **Capital budgeting**: decision rule to answer questions about whether or not to undertake an investment project and to rank various investment projects

A. **Net Present Value for Investment Decisions: The Two-Period Case**
1. **Net present value (NPV)**: value today of all the net cash flows of the investment discounted at the rate of interest.
2. **Separation theorem**: if capital markets are perfect and costless, then individuals' production and consumption decisions can be kept completely separate

B. **Net Present Value Rule of Investment Decisions: The Multiperiod Case**
1. When there are cash flows over more than two periods, the NPV is the sum of the net cash flows discounted at the rate of interest.
2. The rule is to undertake projects if their NPV is positive, or to undertake them in order of their NPVs.
3. Complications may arise if projects are interdependent, if it is difficult to accurately forecast the future stream of net cash flows, or if the firm does not have the resources or is not willing to borrow to undertake all the projects with a positive NPV (it would then choose those with the highest NPV)

16.4 DETERMINANTS OF THE MARKET RATES OF INTEREST

1. **Default risk**: possibility that the loan will not be repaid
2. **Variability risk**: possibility that the yield or return on an investment may vary considerably above or below the average
3. **Real rate of interest (r)**: premium on a unit of a commodity or real consumption income today compared to a unit of the commodity or real consumption income in the future

4. **Nominal rate of interest (r')**: premium on a unit of a monetary claim today compared to a unit of a monetary claim in the future. It is equal to the real rate of interest plus the anticipated rate of price inflation.

16.5 **THE COST OF CAPITAL**
   A. **The Cost of Debt**: return that lenders require to lend their funds to the firm
   B. **The Cost of Equity Capital: The Risk-Free Rate Plus Premium**
      1. The risk-free rate is usually taken to be the six-month U.S. Treasury Bill rate
      2. The premium has two components; the first results from the added risk in investing in the securities of a firm (as opposed to the government) and the second results from the added risk of buying the stock instead of the bonds of the firm
   C. **The Cost of Equity Capital: The Dividend Valuation Model**
      1. **Dividend valuation model**: with perfect information, the value of a share of the common stock of a firm should be equal to the present value of all future dividends expected to be paid on the stock, discounted at the investor's required rate of return
   D. **The Cost of Equity Capital: The Capital Asset Pricing Model (CAPM)**
      1. **Capital asset pricing model (CAPM)**: method commonly used to estimate the equity cost of capital which takes into consideration not only the risk differential between common stocks and government securities, but also the risk differential between the common stock of the firm and the average common stock of all firms or broad-based market portfolios
      2. **Beta coefficient (ß)**: risk differential between the common stock of a particular firm and the common stock of all firms; it is the ratio of the variability in the return of the common stock of the firm to the variability in the average return on the common stocks of all firms.
   E. **The Weighted Cost of Capital**
      1. **Composite cost of capital**: weighted average of the cost of debt capital and equity capital

16.6 **EFFECTS OF FOREIGN INVESTMENTS ON THE RECEIVING NATION**
Foreign investments reduce the supply of investment funds in the investing nation and increase them in the receiving nation. Investments flow to nations with higher rates of return.

16.7 **SOME APPLICATIONS OF FINANCIAL MICROECONOMICS**
   A. **Investment in Human Capital**: any activity on the part of a worker or potential worker that increases his or her productivity, including expenditures on education, job training, health, migration to areas of better job opportunities, and so on
   B. **Investment in Human Capital and Hours of Work**: people may work more hours as a result of investment in human capital; having made the investment in education, the individual will work more hours and earn a higher income to maximize utility

C. **Pricing of Exhaustible Resources**
   1. **Exhaustible resources**: those which are available in fixed quantities and are nonreplenishable (examples include petroleum and minerals)
   2. **Nonexhaustible resources**: those which can last forever if they are properly managed (examples include forests and fish)
D. **Management of Nonexhaustible Resources**
   1. The resource will never be depleted unless the rate of utilization exceeds its rate of natural growth

---

⌘ AT THE FRONTIER ⌘
DERIVATIVES: USEFUL BUT DANGEROUS

Derivatives are financial instruments or contracts whose value is derived from the price of such underlying assets such as stocks, bonds, commodities, and currencies. Used properly, they can be a useful risk-management tool; used without a clear understanding of all their implications, they can be very dangerous and lead to huge losses.

PART III: KEY CONCEPTS IN THIS CHAPTER

1. The _____ is a combination of income received this period and next period, whereas the _____ is the individual's income or endowment this year plus the present value of next year's income or endowment.
2. The premium received by an individual next year by lending money today is the _____ of _____ that is determined at the _____ point between demand and supply in the loanable funds market.
3. The decision rule to rank various investment projects is _____. The _____ is today's value of all the net cash flows of the investment project.
4. If capital markets are perfect and costless, then individuals' production and consumption decisions can be kept completely **complementary/separate**. This idea refers to the _____ theorem.
5. Among the determinants of the market rates of interest are the _____ risk and the _____ risk. The possibility that the loan will not be repaid is the _____ whereas the possibility that the yield or return on the investment will vary considerably above or below the average is the _____.
6. The _____ rate of interest is the premium on a unit of a commodity or _____ consumption income today compared to a unit of the commodity or _____ consumption income in the future. The _____ interest rate is the premium on a unit of a monetary claim today compared to a unit of a monetary claim in the future.
7. The risk-free rate plus premium, meaning the risk-free rate based on the six-month U.S. Treasury Bill rate plus premium, is the _____ of _____, whereas the return that lenders require to lend their funds to the firm constitutes the _____ of _____ to the firm.
8. If the appropriate rate of interest is 8% per year, the approximate present value of an expected $100 million in benefits to be received 2 years from now from selling the

output of a machine is $_____million. If acquiring such a machine costs the firm \$87 million, the firm **should/should not** buy the machine.

9. If the appropriate rate of interest is 6% per year, the approximate present value of an expected \$100 million in benefits to be received 2 years from now from selling the output of a machine is \$_____ million. If acquiring such a machine costs the firm \$87 million, the firm **should/should not** buy the machine. Comparing this answer to that of question 8, we can conclude that a decrease in the interest rate **increases/decreases** the present value of a given investment.

10. You want to start your own business when you complete your college education in four years and your parents are willing to lend you the money for a 30% interest in the business. They want to know how much to deposit in the bank today to make sure you have \$1 million in four years. Knowing that the current interest rate is 10%, you would tell them to deposit \$_____.

11. A firm can invest \$100 million in a four year U.S. government note and receive \$121.55 million, or invest the same sum in a Brazilian corporation and receive \$141.16 million in four years. The total risk factor (default and variability) of investing in the Brazilian corporation is _____%.

12. A firm can invest \$4.5 million in Great Britain and anticipate a return of \$2 million for the next three years. Knowing that the current nominal interest rate is 8%, the net present value for the project is approximately _____.

13. Based on the data given in question 12, a firm **should/should not** invest in the British project. In general, firms should invest in a project when its net present value is _____.

14. If you wanted to ensure that you had \$25 million to start a business when you graduated in three years, you would put approximately _____ million in the bank today knowing that the bank pays 5% per year.

15. A firm can invest \$0.5 million initially and anticipate a stream of flows of \$0.2 million for the next three years. Knowing that the current nominal interest rate is 7%, the net present value for the project is approximately _____.

16. A firm invests \$10 million in Morocco and receives \$15 million after six years. The firm received an interest rate of approximately _____.

17. The method commonly used to estimate the equity cost of capital which takes into consideration not only the risk differential between common stocks and government securities, but also the risk differential between the common stock of the firm and the average common stock of all firms or broad-based market portfolios is the _____ model.

18. _____ is the risk differential between the common stock of a particular firm and the common stock of all firms.

19. Foreign investments tend to **reduce/increase** the supply of investment funds in the investing nation and to **reduce/increase** them in the receiving nation.

20. A nonexhaustible resource will never be depleted unless the rate of utilization is **lower than/equal to/greater than** its rate of natural growth.

PART IV: MULTIPLE-CHOICE QUESTIONS

____1. What is assumed when a consumer has an endowment position?
   a. The consumer has an annuity into perpetuity.
   b. The consumer knows how much of a commodity will be received in the present and in the future.
   c. The government provides a guaranteed income base.
   d. The consumer will have more to consume next year than in the present year.

____2. An individual's wealth (W_0) is given by:
   a. $Y_0 + [Y_1/(1 + r)]$, where Y_0 is income this year, Y_1 is income next year, and r is the interest rate.
   b. $P_1/(1 + r)$, where P_1 is a price next period.
   c. $(C_1 - Y_1)/(C_0 - Y_0)$, where C_0 is consumption this year and C_1 is consumption next year.
   d. $P_0/(1 + r)$, where P_0 is a price this period.

____3. Saving refers to:
   a. the amount of money in a bank account.
   b. the formation of new capital assets.
   c. consuming this period.
   d. the act of refraining from present consumption.

____4. The net present value (NPV) of an investment with a two-period time horizon is given by:
   a. $Y_0 + [Y_1/(1 + r)]$, where Y_0 is income this year, Y_1 is income next year, and r is the interest rate.
   b. $(C_1 - Y_1)/(C_0 - Y_0)$, where C_0 is consumption this year and C_1 is consumption next year.
   c. $-C + (R_1)/(1 + r)$, where $-C$ is the capital investment cost in the current year and R_1 is the net cash flow next year.
   d. $R(1 - t)$, where t is the firm's marginal tax rate.

____5. Default risk refers to:
   a. the possibility that the loan will not be repaid.
   b. the possibility that the yield on an investment may vary considerably around the average yield.
   c. a type of insurance.
   d. the highest variance in returns to be expected from an investment.

____6. The after-tax cost of borrowed funds to a firm is given by:
   a. $r_f + r_p$, where r_f is the risk-free interest rate and r_p is a risk premium.
   b. $r(1 - t)$, where r is the interest rate and t is the firm's marginal tax rate.
   c. $Y_0 + [Y_1/(1 + r)]$, where Y_0 is income this year, Y_1 is income next year, and r is the interest rate.
   d. $P_0/(1 + r)$, where P_0 is a price this period.

____7. If the market rate of interest (r) is 12% with foreign investments in the domestic economy of $100 billion, then:
   a. increased foreign investment will cause the interest rate to increase.
   b. decreased foreign investment will cause the interest rate to decrease.
   c. increased foreign investment will cause the interest rate to decrease.
   d. new foreign investment will have no effect on the interest rate.

____8. Expenditures on education, job training, health, and migration to areas of better job opportunities refers to investment in:
   a. social welfare.
   b. physical capital.
   c. human capital.
   d. financial capital.

____9. Fertile land, forests, rivers and fish are classified as:
   a. nonexhaustible resources, if they are properly managed.
   b. exhaustible resources that are nonreplenishable.
   c. capital.
   d. raw materials.

____10. One of the benefits of foreign investments in the domestic economy is that:
   a. the funds cannot be withdrawn.
   b. technology cannot be transferred abroad.
   c. they help assure domestic control over political and economic matters.
   d. they help finance budget deficits without the need for higher interest rates and more crowding out of private investments.

____11. The cost of equity capital as estimated by the dividend valuation model, gives the present value of a share of common stock to the firm (P) as:
   a. $0.27, if the dividend per share (D) is $3 and the investor's required rate of return (k_e) is 9%.
   b. $33.33, if D = $3 and k_e is 9%.
   c. $0.03, if D = $3 k_e is 9%.
   d. Cannot be calculated with the information provided.

____12. If the real rate of interest (r) is 3%, then:
   a. the nominal rate of interest (r') is 2% if the anticipated rate of inflation (i) is 1%.
   b. r' is 4% if i = 1%.
   c. r' is 0.33% if i = 1%.
   d. r' is 3% if i = 1%.

____13. A given sum (R) of $100 received each year into perpetuity will have the present discounted value (PDV) of:
   a. $2 if the interest rate (r) is 5%.
   b. $100 if r = 1%.
   c. $2000 if r = 5%.
   d. $5000 if r = 5%.

____14. A saving-investment equilibrium without borrowing or lending can be shown with:
   a. isocost-isoquant analysis.
   b. an indifference curve and isocost line.
   c. an isoquant curve and a budget line.
   d. a production possibilities curve and an indifference curve.

____15. The rate of interest (r) is:
   a. the premium received today for borrowing today.
   b. the discount which must be paid for lending today.
   c. profit.
   d. the premium received next year for lending today.

____16. A saving-investment analysis with borrowing or lending has the rate of interest (r) measured as the slope of the:
   a. market line.
   b. production-possibilities curve.
   c. indifference curve.
   d. isocost line.

____17. For a two-period time horizon, net present value (NPV) is:
   a. $54.55, if the capital investment cost (C) is $50, the net cash flow next year (R_1) is $60, and the rate of interest (r) is 10%.
   b. $4.55, if C =$50, R_1 = $60, and r =10%.
   c. -$50.00, if C =$50, R_1 = $60, and r =10%.
   d. $104.55, if C =$50, R_1 = $60, and r =10%.

____18. Variability risk refers to:
   a. the possibility that the loan will not be repaid.
   b. the possibility that the yield on an investment may vary considerably around the average yield.
   c. that risk that cannot be covered by insurance.
   d. the lowest variance in returns to be expected from an investment.

____19. If the cost of capital (k_e) is 12%, then:
   a. the risk premium (r_p) is 17% if the risk-free rate (r_f) is 5%.
   b. r_p is 5% if r_f = 17%.
   c. r_p is 7% if r_f = 5%.
   d. r_p / r_f = 1.

____20. In indifference curve analysis with daily wage on the vertical axis and hours of leisure on the horizontal axis, investment in education is most likely to:
   a. shift the entire budget line parallel toward the origin.
   b. change the horizontal axis intercept of the budget line.
   c. change the vertical axis intercept of the budget line.
   d. change the slope of the indifference map.

____21. In the study of management of nonexhaustible resources, trees should be harvested when:
   a. the rate of growth in the value of standing trees ($\Delta V/V$) equals the market rate of interest (r).
   b. $(\Delta V/V) < r$.
   c. $(\Delta V/V) > r$.
   d. they are in demand.

____22. What does beta (β) represent in the capital asset pricing model (CAPM)?
   a. the average return on all common stocks
   b. the return on government securities
   c. the cost of equity capital to the firm
   d. the risk differential between the common stock of a particular firm and the common stocks of all firms

____23. If the nominal rate of interest (r') is 7%, then:
   a. the real rate of interest (r) is 10% if the rate of inflation (i) is 3%.
   b. r is 4% if i is 3%.
   c. r is 3% if i is 7%.
   d. r is 7% if i is 3%.

____24. In benefit-cost analysis of an investment project, the present value coefficient is:
   a. $P_0(1 + R)$, where P_0 is a price this period and r is the interest rate.
   b. $r(1 - t)$, where t is the firm's marginal tax rate.
   c. $r_f + r_p$, where r_f is the risk-free interest rate and r_p is the risk premium.
   d. $1/(1 + r)^n$, where n is the number of years.

____25. At a rate of interest (r) above equilibrium, there will be an excess quantity:
   a. demanded of lending over the quantity supplied of borrowing.
   b. quantity supplied of borrowing over the quantity demanded of lending.
   c. supplied of lending over the quantity demanded of borrowing.
   d. demanded of borrowing over the quantity supplied of lending.

Use Figure 16-1 to answer questions 26 – 30:

FIGURE 16-1

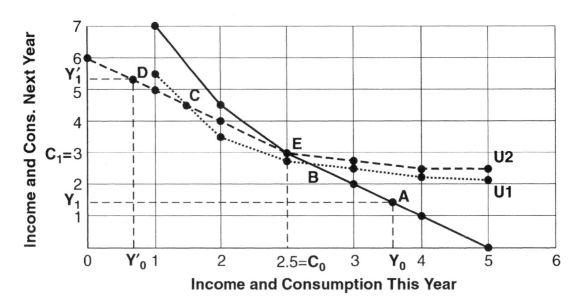

___26. At point A there is:
   a. more income (Y) this year than next.
   b. less Y this year than next.
   c. equilibrium.
   d. maximum satisfaction.

___27. At point D there is:
   a. more income (Y) this year than next.
   b. less Y this year than next.
   c. equilibrium.
   d. maximum satisfaction.

___28. What do points B and C have in common?
   a. more income (Y) this year than next
   b. less Y this year than next
   c. equilibrium
   d. disequilibrium

___29 In order to move from point A to point E the consumer must:
   a. borrow $Y_1 - C_1$ units from next year's endowment to use the same amount next year.
   b. lend $C_1 - Y_1$ units from this year's endowment and receive $Y_0 - C_0$ additional units next year.
   c. lend $Y_0 - C_0$ units from this year's endowment and receive $C_1 - Y_1$ additional units next year.
   d. borrow $Y_1 - C_1$ units from next year's endowment to use $Y_0 - C_0$ units next year.

___30. In order to move from point D to point E, the consumer must:

a. borrow $Y_0' - C_0$ units from this year's endowment by repaying the same amount next year.

b. lend $Y_1' - C_1$ units from this year's endowment and receive the same amount next year.

c. lend $Y_1 - C_0$ units from this year's endowment and receive $Y_1' - C_1$ units next year.

d. borrow $C_0 - Y_0'$ units from this year's endowment and repay $Y_1' - C_1$ units next year.

CHAPTER 17:

GENERAL EQUILIBRIUM AND WELFARE ECONOMICS

PART I: REVIEW OF CONCEPTS FROM PREVIOUS CHAPTER

Prior to reading chapter 17, match statements at left with the appropriate concept at right.

____1. Value today of all the net cash flows of an investment
____2. Determines price of goods and services
____3. Revenues net of total costs
____4. Factor demand curve
____5. These are zero at the break-even point
____6. Contrary to explicit costs
____7. Goods with negative cross elasticity of demand
____8. A movement along a supply curve is a change in this
____9. Dollar outlays to acquire inputs
____10. Additional production per additional unit of an input
____11. Highest benefits foregone when taking an action
____12. Decision rule to rank various investment projects
____13. Profit-maximizing rule from the input side
____14. Possibility that a loan will not be repaid
____15. Possibility that the return on an investment may vary
     considerably above or below the average

a. implicit costs
b. opportunity costs
c. MRP curve
d. market
e. explicit costs
f. MRP = ME
g. NPV
h. capital budgeting
i. complements
j. marginal product
k. profits
l. economic profits
m. quantity supplied
n. variability risk
o. default risk

PART II: ANNOTATED CHAPTER OUTLINE

17.1 PARTIAL VERSUS GENERAL EQUILIBRIUM ANALYSIS
1. **Partial equilibrium analysis**: study of the behavior of individual decision-making units and individual markets, viewed in isolation
2. **General equilibrium analysis**: studies the interdependence that exists among all markets and prices in the economy, meaning how changes in any market can have spillover effects on other markets, which in turn have repercussions or feedback effects on the original market
3. **Interdependence**: interconnections among all markets and prices in the economy

17.2   GENERAL EQUILIBRIUM OF EXCHANGE AND PRODUCTION
A. General Equilibrium of Exchange
1. **Edgeworth box diagram for exchange**: represents two individuals each exchanging two goods. Any point inside the box indicates how the total amount of the two goods is distributed between the two individuals.
2. **Contract curve for exchange**: locus of tangency points of the indifference curves of two individuals. Along this curve the marginal rate of substitution of X for Y (MRS_{XY}) is the same for the two individuals A and B, and hence the economy is in general equilibrium of exchange
B. General Equilibrium of Production
1. **Edgeworth box diagram for production**: represents two commodities, each produced with two inputs. Any point inside the box indicates how the total amount of the two inputs is utilized in the production of the two commodities.
2. **Contract curve for production**: locus of tangency points of the isoquants for X and Y at which the marginal rate of technical substitution of labor for capital ($MRTS_{LK}$) in the production of X and Y are equal and the economy is in general equilibrium of production.
C. Derivation of the Production-Possibilities Frontier
1. **Production-possibilities frontier**: also called the transformation curve, it shows the various combinations of commodities X and Y that the economy can produce by fully utilizing all of the fixed amounts of labor and capital with the best technology available
2. **Marginal rate of transformation of X for Y (MRT_{XY})**: amount of commodity Y that the economy must give up, at a particular point on the production-possibilities frontier, so as to release just enough labor and capital to produce one additional unit of commodity X

17.3   GENERAL EQUILIBRIUM OF PRODUCTION AND EXCHANGE AND PARETO OPTIMALITY
A. General Equilibrium of Production and Exchange Simultaneously
1. The marginal rate of transformation between the two commodities must be equal to the marginal rate of substitution of the same two commodities for two individuals
B. Marginal Conditions for Economic Efficiency and Pareto Optimality
1. **Economic efficiency**: it is maximum with general equilibrium of production and exchange
2. **Pareto optimality**: when no reorganization of production and consumption is possible by which some individuals are made better off without making someone else worse off

17.4   PERFECT COMPETITION, ECONOMIC EFFICIENCY, AND EQUITY
A. Perfect Competition and Economic Efficiency
With perfect competition in all input and commodity markets, the three marginal conditions for economic efficiency or Pareto optimum in production and exchange are automatically satisfied

B. Efficiency and Equity

1. **Law of the invisible hand**: in a free market economy, when each individual is pursuing his or her own selfish interests, he or she is also led to promote the well-being of society, more so than he or she intends or even understands

2. **First theorem of welfare economics**: equilibrium produced by competitive markets exhaust all possible gains from exchange or that equilibrium in competitive markets is Pareto optimal

3. **Second theorem of welfare economics**: when indifference curves are convex to their origin, every efficient allocation (every point on the contract curve for exchange) is a competitive equilibrium for some initial allocation of goods or distribution of inputs (income)

4. **Market failures**: arise in the presence of imperfect competition, externalities, and public goods

17.5 GENERAL EQUILIBRIUM OF PRODUCTION AND EXCHANGE WITH INTERNATIONAL TRADE

A. General Equilibrium with International Trade

1. **Comparative advantage**: given the same technology and tastes in two nations, the cost of producing an additional unit of X is lower in one nation than in the other

17.6 WELFARE ECONOMICS AND UTILITY-POSSIBILITY FRONTIERS

A. The Meaning of Welfare Economics

1. **Welfare economics**: studies the conditions under which the solution to the general equilibrium model can be said to be optimal

B. Utility-Possibilities Frontier

1. **Utility-possibilities frontier**: shows the various combinations of utilities received by individuals A and B when this simple economy is in general equilibrium or Pareto optimum in exchange

C. Grand Utility-Possibilities Frontier

1. **Grand utility-possibilities frontier**: envelope to the utility-possibilities frontiers at Pareto optimum points of production and exchange

17.7 SOCIAL POLICY CRITERIA

A. Measuring Changes in Social Welfare

1. **Pareto criterion**: a policy increases social welfare if it benefits some members of society without harming anyone

2. **Compensation principle or Kaldor-Hicks criterion**: a change is an improvement if those who gain from the change can fully compensate the losers and still retain some gain

3. **Scitovsky criterion**: a double Kaldor-Hicks test; that is, a change is an improvement if it satisfies the Kaldor-Hicks criterion and, after the change, a movement back to the original position does not satisfy the Kaldor-Hicks criterion.

4. **Bergson social welfare function**: a particular policy is said to increase social welfare if it puts society on a higher social indifference curve
   B. **Arrow's Impossibility Theorem**: social welfare function cannot be derived by democratic vote

17.8 TRADE PROTECTION AND ECONOMIC WELFARE

Since trade protection benefits domestic producers and harms domestic consumers there is a bias in favor of protectionism.

⌘ AT THE FRONTIER ⌘
THE HOT ISSUE OF INCOME INEQUALITY IN THE UNITED STATES

The best-known summary measure of income inequality is provided by the **Lorenz curve** and the **Gini coefficient**. A Lorenz curve shows the cumulative percentages of total income measured along the vertical axis for various cumulative percentages of the population measured along the horizontal axis. The Gini coefficient is given by the ratio of the area between the Lorenz curve and the straight-line diagonal to the total area of triangle formed under the diagonal. The Gini coefficient can range from 0 (perfect equality) to 1 (perfect inequality).

PART III: KEY CONCEPTS IN THIS CHAPTER

1. The study of behavior of individual decision-making units and individual markets, viewed in isolation, is called _____ analysis.

2. The interconnections among all markets and prices in the economy reflects the phenomenon of _____. The study of such interconnections is called _____ analysis.

3. The locus of tangency points of the indifference curves of two individuals is the _____ for _____.

4. The locus of tangency points of the isoquants for goods X and Y at which the marginal rate of technical substitution of labor for capital in the production of X and Y are equal is the _____ for _____.

5. The _____ shows the various combinations of goods X and Y that the economy can produce by fully utilizing all of the fixed amounts of labor and capital with the best technology available.

6. The _____ of _____ of X for Y reflects the amount of commodity Y that the economy must give up, at a particular point on the production-possibilities frontier, so as to release just enough labor and capital to produce one additional unit of commodity X.

7. The _____ diagram for _____ represents two individuals, each exchanging two goods, whereas the _____ for _____ represents two commodities, each produced with two inputs.

8. The general equilibrium of production and exchange simultaneously is reached when the _____ between two commodities is **lower than/equal to/greater than** the _____ of the same two commodities for two individuals.

9. _____ is reached when the general equilibrium of production and exchange is achieved.

10. The condition of _____ is that no reorganization of production and consumption is possible by which some individuals are made better off without making someone else worse off.

11. Adam Smith advocated the law of the _____, meaning that in a free market economy, when each individual is pursuing his or her own selfish interests, he or she is also led to promote the well-being of society, more so than he or she intends or even understands.

12. _____ economics studies the conditions under which the solution to the general equilibrium model can be said to be optimal.

13. There are _____ theorems of welfare economics. The first one is that an equilibrium produced by competitive markets exhausts all possible gains from exchange: such an equilibrium is _____. The second one is that indifference curves are _____ to the origin. Every efficient allocation is a _____ for some initial allocation of goods or distribution of inputs (income).

14. Market failures arise in the presence of _____, _____, and _____.

15. The _____ frontier shows the various combinations under which the solution to the general equilibrium model can be said to be optimal.

16. The envelope to the utility-possibilities frontiers at Pareto optimum points of production and exchange is called the _____ frontier.

17. Given the same technology and tastes in two nations, when one nation has a lower cost of producing an additional unit of X than the other it has a _____ over the other nation.

18. There is bias **in favor of/against** protectionism since trade protection **benefits/harms** domestic consumers and **benefits/harms** domestic producers.

19. _____ reflects the idea that the social welfare function cannot be derived by democratic votes.

20. Measuring changes in social welfare can be done using the _____ criterion, which defines a change as an improvement if those who gain from the change can fully compensate the losers and still retain some gain.

PART IV: MULTIPLE-CHOICE QUESTIONS

___1. General equilibrium studies the:
   a. interdependence or interconnections that exist among all markets.
   b. individual decision-making units.
   c. individual markets viewed in isolation.
   d. generalizations reached through inductive reasoning.

____2. The general equilibrium of exchange for an economy with two individuals, two commodities, and no production can be illustrated by the:
    a. production-possibilities frontier.
    b. utility-possibilities frontier.
    c. Edgeworth box diagram for exchange.
    d. Edgeworth box diagram for production.

____3. When there is general equilibrium of production and exchange, and economic efficiency is maximum, it is a(n):
    a. example of the law of the invisible hand.
    b. situation of Pareto optimality.
    c. application of Arrow's Impossibility Theorem.
    d. application of the Bergson Social Welfare Function.

____4. In a graphic analysis of general equilibrium with international trade of two countries and two goods, trade will be determined where:
    a. the marginal rate of transformation of good X for good Y ($MRTS_{XY}$) is equal to P_Y/P_X.
    b. MRT_{XY} is equal to P_X/P_Y.
    c. MRT_{XY} is equal to the marginal rate of technical substitution of good X for good Y ($MRTS_{XY}$).
    d. MRT_{XY} is equal to the marginal rate of substitution of good Y for good Y (MRS_{XY}).

____5. The first theorem of welfare economics is:
    a. when indifference curves are convex to their origin, every efficient allocation is a competitive equilibrium for some initial allocation of goods or distribution of inputs (income).
    b. when indifference curves are concave to their origin, every efficient allocation is a competitive equilibrium for some initial allocation of goods or distribution of inputs (income).
    c. that an equilibrium produced by competitive markets exhausts all possible gains from exchange, but that equilibrium in competitive markets is not Pareto optimal.
    d. that an equilibrium produced by competitive markets exhausts all possible gains from exchange, or that equilibrium in competitive markets is Pareto optimal.

____6. Welfare economics studies the:
    a. history of the government programs which provide aid to low-income families.
    b. profit maximization of individual firms in isolation.
    c. utility maximization of individual consumers in isolation.
    d. conditions under which the solution to the general equilibrium model can be said to be optimal.

____7. Which of the following states that a policy must increase social welfare if it benefits some members of society without harming anyone?
   a. Kaldor-Hicks criterion
   b. Scitovsky criterion
   c. Pareto criterion
   d. Law of invisible hand

____8. Which theory postulates that industries that are highly organized receive more trade protection than those that are less organized?
   a. Arrow's Impossibility Theorem
   b. pressure-group or interest-group theory
   c. infant industry theory
   d. Pareto theory

____9. Which of the following states that a social welfare function cannot be derived by a democratic vote?
   a. Arrow's Impossibility Theorem
   b. the fourth criterion of welfare economics
   c. Scitovsky criterion
   d. Kaldor-Hicks criterion

____10. The envelope of the utility-possibilities frontiers at Pareto optimum points of production and exchange is the _____ frontier.
   a. grand utility-possibilities
   b. utility-possibilities
   c. production-possibilities
   d. consumption-possibilities

____11. For economic efficiency and Pareto optimum to be reached, there should be:
   a. imperfect competition in input and output markets.
   b. externalities and diseconomies of scale.
   c. public goods which replace private goods.
   d. no market failures.

____12. In the case of two goods, X and Y, and two consumers, A and B, Pareto optimality in production and consumption requires that the:
   a. marginal rate of transformation of X for Y (MRT_{XY}) equal the marginal rate of substitution of X for Y (MRS_{XY}).
   b. MRT_{XY} equal the MRS XY for both individuals.
   c. $MRT_{XY} = P_Y = P_X$.
   d. marginal rate of technical substitution of A for B ($MRTS_{AB}$) be equal for the two commodities X and Y.

____13. The absolute value of the slope of the production-possibilities frontier is the:
   a. marginal rate of technical substitution (MRTS).
   b. marginal rate of transformation (MRT).
   c. marginal rate of substitution (MRS).
   d. ratio of two input prices.

____14. The locus of the tangency points of the indifference curves for two individuals is the:
   a. grand utility-possibilities frontier.
   b. utility-possibilities frontier.
   c. contract curve for exchange.
   d. consumption-possibilities frontier.

____15. In the case of efficiency in production and exchange in a "Robinson Crusoe" economy, if the marginal rate of transformation of good X for good Y (MRT_{XY}) is:
   a. greater than the marginal rate of substitution of X for Y (MRS_{XY}), then the adjustment to equilibrium would require less X and more Y.
   b. greater than the MRS_{XY}, then the adjustment to equilibrium would require more X and less Y.
   c. less than the MRS_{XY}, then the adjustment to equilibrium would require less X and more Y.
   d. the same as the MRS_{XY}, then the adjustment to equilibrium would require more X and less Y.

____16. Which of the following postulates that in a free market economy, each individual by pursuing his or her own selfish interest is led to promote the well-being of society?
   a. first theorem of welfare economics
   b. second theorem of welfare economics
   c. Law of the invisible hand
   d. Arrow's Impossibility Theorem

____17. The locus of maximum utility for one individual for any given level of utility for another individual is the:
   a. grand utility-possibilities frontier.
   b. utility-possibilities frontier.
   c. contract curve for exchange.
   d. consumption-possibilities frontier.

____18. Which of the following states that a change is an improvement if those who gain from the change can fully compensate the losers and still retain some gain?
   a. Arrow's Impossibility Theorem
   b. the fourth criterion of welfare economics
   c. Scitovsky criterion
   d. Kaldor-Hicks criterion

____19. Assume a grand utility-possibilities frontier which intersects the vertical axis at $U_B = 350$ and intersects the horizontal axis at $U_A = 450$, where U_A and U_B are the total utilities for two individuals A and B. Which of the following is true?
   a. Interpersonal comparisons of utility can be made, and therefore social welfare must change as you move along the curve.
   b. All points above the curve are achievable levels of social welfare, *ceteris paribus*.

c. From a point to the interior of the curve, a 90 degree triangle with legs parallel to the vertical axis and horizontal axis will mark two points on the curve in between which both individuals can move and benefit and harm no one.

d. From a point to the interior of the curve, a 90 degree triangle with legs parallel to the vertical axis and horizontal axis will mark two points on the curve in between which both individuals can move and benefit but at least one other individual is harmed.

___20. In the case of efficiency in production and exchange in a "Robinson Crusoe" economy, if the marginal rate of substitution of good X for good Y (MRS$_{XY}$) is:

a. greater than the marginal rate of transformation of X for Y (MRT$_{XY}$), then the adjustment to equilibrium would require less X and more Y.

b. greater than the MRT$_{XY}$, then the adjustment to equilibrium would require more X and less Y.

c. the same as the MRT$_{XY}$, then the adjustment to equilibrium would require less X and more Y.

d. less than the MRT$_{XY}$, then the adjustment to equilibrium would require more X and less Y.

___21. With good X on the horizontal axis and good Y on the vertical axis for a production-possibilities frontier, as one substitutes X for Y:

a. the marginal rate of transformation of X for Y (MRT$_{XY}$) increases.

b. the MRT$_{XY}$ decreases.

c. the MRT$_{XY}$ is constant.

d. the MRS$_{XY}$ increases.

___22. The locus of the tangency points of the isoquants is the:

a. grand utility-possibilities frontier.

b. utility-possibilities frontier.

c. contract curve for production.

d. consumption-possibilities frontier.

___23. In an Edgeworth box diagram for production, if the marginal rate of technical substitution of labor for capital (MRTS$_{LK}$) in the production of good X is:

a. equal to the marginal rate of technical substitution of labor for capital (MRTS$_{LK}$) in the production of good Y, then the firms are on the contract curve for production.

b. equal to the marginal rate of technical substitution of labor for capital (MRTS$_{LK}$) in the production of good Y, then the firms are on the contract curve for exchange.

c. not equal to the marginal rate of technical substitution of labor for capital (MRTS$_{LK}$) in the production of good Y, then no further adjustments are necessary.

d. not equal to the marginal rate of technical substitution of labor for capital (MRTS$_{LK}$) in the production of good Y, then both firms should increase the production of good X.

____24. In an Edgeworth box diagram for exchange, if the marginal rate of substitution of good X for good Y ($MRTS_{XY}$) for individual A is:

    a. greater than the marginal rate of substitution of good X for good Y (MRS_{XY}) for individual B, then the individuals are on the contract curve for exchange.

    b. equal to the marginal rate of substitution of good X for good Y (MRS_{XY}) for individual B, then the individuals are on the contract curve for exchange.

    c. not equal to the marginal rate of substitution of good X for good Y (MRS_{XY}) for individual B, then no further adjustments are necessary.

    d. not equal to the marginal rate of substitution of good X for good Y (MRS_{XY}) for individual B, then both individuals should increase the consumption of good X.

____25. Partial equilibrium analysis studies the:

    a. interdependence or interconnections that exist among all markets.

    b. aggregate decision-making units.

    c. markets viewed in dynamic continuous exchange.

    d. individual markets viewed in isolation.

Use Figure 17-1 to answer questions 26 – 30:

FIGURE 17-1

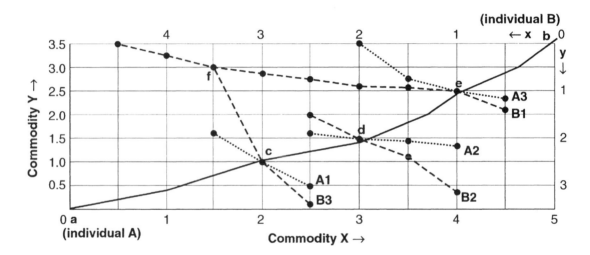

____26. What type of diagram is shown in Figure 17-1?

    a. production-possibilities frontier

    b. utility-possibilities frontier

    c. Edgeworth box for production

    d. Edgeworth box for exchange

____27. Line cde is:

    a. the contract curve for production.

    b. the contract curve for exchange.

    c. the locus of isoquant tangencies.

    d. the utility-possibilities frontier.

___28. At point c, the marginal rate of substitution of good X for good Y (MRS_{XY}) for individual A is:

a. greater than the marginal rate of substitution of good X for good Y (MRS_{XY}) for individual B.

b. less than the marginal rate of substitution of good X for good Y (MRS_{XY}) for individual B.

c. equal to the marginal rate of substitution of good X for good Y (MRS_{XY}) for individual B.

d. constant and equal to one.

___29 As one moves from point c to point e the marginal rate of substitution of good X for good Y (MRS_{XY}) for individual A:

a. decreases.

b. increases.

c. is constant.

d. is no longer equal to the marginal rate of substitution of good X for good Y (MRS_{XY}) for individual B.

___30. Starting at the intersection point of A1 and B1, a movement to point c or point e results in a:

a. gain in utility for both individuals.

b. gain in utility for one individual without the other losing utility.

c. loss in utility for both individuals.

d. gain in utility for one individual and a loss by the other.

CHAPTER 18:

EXTERNALITIES, PUBLIC GOODS, AND THE ROLE OF GOVERNMENT

Prior to reading chapter 18, match statements at left with the appropriate concept at right.

____1. Mandatory charge levied by government
____2. Satisfaction from consuming a good
____3. Interconnections among all markets and prices in the economy
____4. Dollar outlays to acquire inputs
____5. Positive results from taking an action
____6. Excess of MRP of the variable input over the input price
____7. The act of giving up something to acquire something else
____8. Goal of private firms
____9. Dollar value a consumer attributes to a good
____10. General equilibrium of production and exchange
____11. Additional cost of producing one more unit
____12. Additional benefit of acquiring one more unit
____13. Condition of distributional efficiency in perfectly competitive markets
____14. Condition of technical efficiency
____15. Policy increases social welfare if it benefits some members of society without harming anyone else

a. utility
b. profit maximization
c. interdependence
d. monopsonistic exploitation
e. exchange
f. costs
g. benefits
h. tax
i. marginal cost
j. P = MC
k. price
l. economic efficiency
m. marginal benefit
n. Pareto optimality
o. P = minimum SAC

PART II: ANNOTATED CHAPTER OUTLINE

18.1   EXTERNALITIES
A. Externalities Defined
1. **Externalities**: side effects that are borne by firms and people not directly involved in the production or consumption of the commodities
2. **External costs**: harmful externalities
3. **External benefits**: beneficial externalities
4. **External diseconomies of production**: uncompensated costs imposed on others by the expansion of output by some firms
5. **External diseconomies of consumption**: uncompensated costs imposed on others by the consumption expenditures of some individuals
6. **External economies of production**: uncompensated benefits conferred on others by the expansion of output by some firms

7. **External economies of consumption**: uncompensated benefits conferred on others by the increased consumption of a commodity by some individual
8. **Technical externalities**: arise when declining long-run average costs (LAC) as output (Q) expands lead to monopoly, so that price (P) exceeds marginal cost (MC)
B. **Externalities and Market Failure**: when externalities are present, Pareto optimum is not achieved even under perfect competition, because private and social costs (and benefits) differ

18.2 EXTERNALITIES AND PROPERTY RIGHTS

1. **Common property**: property for which there is no clear owner (such as air)
2. **Coase theorem**: postulates that when property rights are clearly defined and transaction costs are zero, perfect competition results in the internalization of externalities, regardless of how property rights are assigned among the parties
3. **Internalizing external costs**: the cost associated with the externality becomes part of the expenses of one or the other of the parties involved. Thus, externalities are avoided under perfect competition, if property rights are clearly defined and transferable, and if transaction costs are zero

18.3 PUBLIC GOODS

A. **Nature of Public Goods**
1. **Public goods**: a commodity for which its consumption by one individual does not reduce the amount available for others
2. **Nonrival consumption**: the distinguishing characteristic of public goods; means that one person's consumption of the good does not diminish the amount available for others to consume
3. **Nonexclusion**: impossible or prohibitively expensive to confine the benefits of the consumption of a good to selected people (such as only those paying for it)
B. **Provision of Public Goods**
1. **Free-rider problem**: each consumer believes that the public good will be provided anyway, whether he or she contributes to its payment or not, and so the consumer does not pay for the good

18.4 BENEFIT-COST ANALYSIS: a useful procedure for determining the most worthwhile projects, this analysis compares the present value of the benefits of a project to the present value of the costs of a project. The project should be carried out if the benefit-cost ratio of the project exceeds 1. However, it is difficult to estimate the benefits and the costs (indeed some of them may not be quantifiable), and to determine the appropriate rate of interest to use to calculate the present value

18.5 THE THEORY OF PUBLIC CHOICE

A. **Meaning and Importance of Public-Choice Theory**
1. **Theory of public choice**: study of how government decisions are made and implemented
2. **Government failures**: situations where government policies do not reflect the public's interests and reduce rather than increase social welfare

B. **The Public-Choice Process**
1. **Voters**: the political counterpart of the consumer in the marketplace
2. **Rational ignorance**: voters are much less informed about political decisions than about their individual market decisions
3. **Politicians**: the political counterpart of entrepreneurs or managers of private firms
4. **Special-interest groups**: pressure groups which seek either to elect politicians or to ensure the passage of certain laws
5. **Bureaucrats**: run the bureaus that carry out the policies enacted by Congress
C. **Policy Implications of Public-Choice Theory**: while public policies can improve the functioning of the economic system in the presence of market failures, the government itself is subject to systematic forces that can lead to government failures. The theory suggests that public-sector performance can be improved by subjecting government agencies to competition whenever possible

18.6 **STRATEGIC TRADE POLICY**: a nation can create a comparative advantage in such fields as semiconductors, computers, telecommunications, and other industries that are deemed crucial to future growth in the nation

18.7 **GOVERNMENT CONTROL AND REGULATION OF ENVIRONMENTAL POLLUTION**
A. **Environmental Pollution**: air pollution, water pollution, thermal pollution, pollution resulting from garbage disposal, and so on
B. **Optimal Pollution Control**: where marginal benefits equal marginal costs
C. **Direct Regulation and Effluent Fees for Optimal Pollution Control**
1. **Effluent fee**: brings the private cost of pollution equal to its social costs

⌘   AT THE FRONTIER   ⌘
EFFICIENCY VERSUS EQUITY IN U.S. TAX REFORM

Europeans pay much higher taxes than Americans, but also get much greater benefits. Recent reform of the U.S. tax system further increased transatlantic differences.

PART III: KEY CONCEPTS IN THIS CHAPTER

1. The side effects that are borne by firms and people not directly involved in the production or consumption of the commodities are **public goods/externalities**. When they are **positive/negative** they are **beneficial/harmful/external** benefits, and they are **positive/negative** when they are **beneficial/harmful/external** costs.
2. Uncompensated costs imposed on others by the expansion of output by some firms are _____ whereas those imposed on others by the consumption expenditures of some individuals are _____.

3. Uncompensated benefits conferred on others by the expansion of output by some firms are _____ whereas those imposed on others by the consumption expenditures are _____.

4. _____ arise when declining long-run average costs as output expands lead to **monopoly/a more competitive firm** so that price **exceeds/equals** the marginal cost.

5. Property to which there is not a clear owner (such as air) is a _____ property. For example, western grazing lands are most likely _____ property; logically, the lands are most likely frequently **overgrazed/undergrazed** by cattle since there **is/is not** a fee to ranchers to graze cattle.

6. The _____ theorem postulates that when property rights are clearly defined and transactions costs are _____, perfect competition results in the internalization of externalities, **contingent upon/regardless of** how property rights are assigned among the parties.

7. The _____ theory postulates that private negotiations via a perfectly competitive market can **internalize/magnify** externalities.

8. _____ external costs means that externalities are avoided under perfect competition, if property rights are clearly defined and **non-transferable/transferable**, and if transactions costs are zero.

9. A _____ good is a commodity for which consumption by one individual does not reduce the amount available for others. Hence, such a good can provide **exclusive/simultaneous** benefits to more than one consumer. This phenomenon is that of _____ consumption, which is one of the distinguishing characteristics of such goods.

10. National defense **is/is not** a nonrival good, whereas a Mustang **is/is not**. A fireworks display **is/is not** a nonrival good, whereas a slice of pizza **is/is not**.

11. _____ means that it is impossible or prohibitively expensive to confine the benefits of the consumption of a good to selected people.

12. Some consumers believe that the public good will be provided anyway, whether or not they contribute to its payment or not. Most likely, they will try to obtain the benefits the public good provided without paying for it. These people are _____.

13. The analysis that compares the present value of benefits to that of the costs of a project is called the _____.

14. Public choice theory applies economic analysis to **business/political/economic** decision-making.

15. The situations where government policies do not reflect the public's interests and reduce rather than increase social welfare are those of _____.

16. The voters are much less informed about political decisions than about their individual market decisions, probably because the ratio of benefit to cost of gathering political information is **higher/lower** than that of gathering market information. Such a description is in line with the choice of _____.

17. Pressure groups that either seek to elect politicians or to ensure the passage of certain laws are _____. These groups tend to exert a **weak/strong** influence on the political process.

18. Although they run the bureaus that carry out policies enacted by Congress, _____ are **elected/unelected** government employees. The characterization of the political process by public-choice theorists is excessively cynical possibly

because interest group members are typically **more/less** informed about issues that affect them than the general public is about the same issues. **Interest group members have/The general public has** a stronger economic incentive to become informed about the issues in question.

19. The optimal pollution control is achieved when the _____ of cleaning up equals its _____.

20. A(n) _____ brings the private cost of pollution equal to its social cost.

PART IV: MULTIPLE-CHOICE QUESTIONS

___1. The harmful or beneficial effects borne by firms and people not directly involved in the production or consumption of the commodities in question are:
  a. externalized in public goods.
  b. internalized in common property.
  c. captured in private goods.
  d. externalities.

___2. When neither firms, governments, nor individuals can own a particular item, it is called:
  a. common property.
  b. private property.
  c. public property.
  d. quasi-private property.

___3. National defense, law enforcement, fire and police protection, and government-provided flood control are examples of:
  a. common property.
  b. private property.
  c. public property.
  d. externalities.

___4. When government agencies must decide which projects to implement and which to reject, they often choose projects which have benefit-cost ratios:
  a. greater than 1.
  b. equal to 1.
  c. equal to 0.
  d. less than 1.

___5. The study of how government decisions are made and implemented is:
  a. price theory.
  b. benefit-cost analysis.
  c. public-choice theory.
  d. the Coase theorem.

_____6. When a nation's government creates a comparative advantage through policies which aid industries that are deemed crucial to the future growth of that nation, there is(are):
  a. a system of free trade.
  b. a policy of no government-industry cooperation.
  c. no tax benefits allowed for those industries.
  d. strategic trade policy.

_____7. Environmental pollution is an example of:
  a. negative externalities.
  b. internal diseconomies of scale.
  c. technical externalities.
  d. a private cost of production.

_____8. Public-choice theory suggests that public sector performance can be improved by:
  a. allowing a public sector monopoly.
  b. regulation of the output of the sector.
  c. subjecting government agencies to competition.
  d. a bilateral monopoly.

_____9. When trying to estimate the benefits and costs of a government project which is estimated to have an active life of 50 years:
  a. it is easy to select the proper interest rate to be used to calculate the present values.
  b. the quantification of the benefits and costs is not important.
  c. the prices included in the analysis always capture the opportunity cost of the outputs from or inputs used for the project.
  d. it is difficult or impossible to estimate the costs and benefits into the future.

_____10. When each consumer believes that a public good will be provided whether or not he or she contributes to its payment there is:
  a. a market-clearing equilibrium.
  b. a free-rider problem.
  c. an optimal amount of the public good.
  d. an adequate funding of the public good without taxation.

_____11. If a firm that is polluting the environment is forced to install a device that will prevent the pollution, there is:
  a. an internalization of the external cost of pollution.
  b. a social cost.
  c. a free-rider problem.
  d. an effluent fee.

_____12. A central city property owners association was concerned because although there was not enough lighting around their businesses, no one seemed interested in paying for more street lamps. This illustrates that, with the free-rider problem:
  a. individual property owners might choose to mask their true demand for the street lamps.
  b. the behavior increases as the size of the group decreases.

    c. private goods are affected but not public goods.

    d. the optimal number of the street lamps is easily determined.

___13. The Coase theorem may not solve market failures when:

    a. the number of parties involved is too small.

    b. transactions costs are low.

    c. the parties involved cannot be easily identified.

    d. transactions costs are high.

___14. When there are external diseconomies of consumption, consumers:

    a. should not be taxed to correct the market distortion.

    b. and producers should be taxed to correct the market distortion.

    c. do not pay the full marginal social cost of the commodity and consume too much of it.

    d. must pay compensation to third parties.

___15. The Coase theorem demonstrates that if property rights are clearly defined and if the number of affected parties is small:

    a. unmodified demand and supply analysis can be used to solve the problem of externalities.

    b. resolution of the externality problem is not possible.

    c. the affected individuals should not take action to solve an externality problem because the transactions costs will be too high.

    d. the affected individuals can take effective action to solve the externality problem.

___16. The distinguishing characteristic of public goods is:

    a. nonexclusion.

    b. nonrival consumption.

    c. the absence of externalities.

    d. market price.

___17. Perhaps the most serious difficulty with benefit-choice analysis is:

    a. the choice of the proper interest rate used to find the present value of the benefits and costs.

    b. the calculation of the benefits and costs.

    c. keeping the ratio of benefits to costs a positive fraction.

    d. keeping the ratio of costs to benefits greater than one.

___18. When public-choice theorists study how the political process and government actually work rather than how they should work, they find:

    a. that voters are not indifferent about most public choices.

    b. that voters are not ignorant about most public choices.

    c. there is a possibility of government failures.

    d. there is an impossibility of government failures.

____19. If the marginal costs (MC) from pollution are $50 and the marginal benefits (MB) of pollution are $45, then:
a. all pollution must stop by ceasing pollution.
b. there can be $5 more of pollution.
c. total benefits of pollution exceed total costs from pollution by $5.
d. pollution can be increased without decreasing net total benefits.

____20. A tax that a firm must pay to the government for discharging waste or otherwise polluting is:
a. an excise tax.
b. an ad valorem tax.
c. an effluent fee.
d. a property tax.

____21. According to public-choice theory, bureaucrats seek to:
a. influence government policies to further their own personal interests.
b. behave as profit maximizers.
c. minimize the costs of operating their bureaus.
d. cut the government debt.

____22. According to public-choice theory, voters have "rational ignorance," which is:
b. being informed about individual purchases made by government.
c. being much less informed about political decisions than about their individual market decisions.
d. having rational expectations.
e. supporting the right to not attend public educational institutions.

____23. "When evaluating a project which will result in energy production with less pollution, how does one place a value on being able to see a mountain range in the absence of pollution?" Such a statement illustrates:
a. an explicit cost associated with the project.
b. a measurable benefit which has a price determined in the market.
c. that some costs and benefits of a project may not be quantifiable.
d. that all costs and benefits of a project are quantifiable.

____24. When a public good is provided for some individuals but other individuals cannot be kept from also enjoying it even though they have not paid for it, there is(are):
a. no free riders.
b. nonrival consumption.
c. exclusive consumption.
d. nonexclusion in consumption.

____25. What can drive a wedge between private and social costs or benefits, and prevent attainment of economic efficiency and Pareto optimality?
a. externalities
b. internalities
c. common property
d. public goods

Use Figure 18-1 to answer questions 26 – 30. The supply curve (S) and demand curve (d) apply to a perfectly competitive market without externalities.

FIGURE 18-1

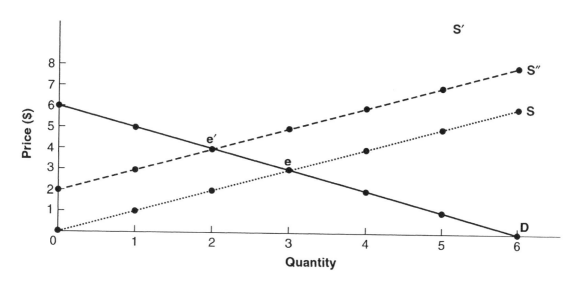

_____26. The supply curve (S) is a measure of:
  a. marginal private costs (MC_P).
  b. marginal external costs (MC_E).
  c. average private costs.
  d. average external costs.

_____27. If the marginal external costs (MC_E) is added to the marginal private costs (MC_P), then a new supply curve is given by S′. What is the MC_E associated with the quantity of good X (Q_X) 2?
  a. $4
  b. ($4 - $2) = $2
  c. ($2 - $0) = $2
  d. ($4)(2) = $8

_____28. When externalities are not included, what is the equilibrium price (P) and quantity (Q_X)?
  a. P = $4 and Q_X = 2
  b. P = $2 and Q_X = 2
  c. P = $3 and Q_X = 3
  d. P = $4 and Q_X = 3

____29 When externalities are included, what is the equilibrium price (P) and quantity (Q_X)?
   a.   P = \$4 and $Q_X = 2$
   b.   P = \$2 and $Q_X = 2$
   c.   P = \$3 and $Q_X = 3$
   d.   P = \$4 and $Q_X = 3$

____30. If a per-unit corrective tax were placed on every level of Q_X, then the supply curve would be:
   a.   S″ with a different equilibrium P and Q_X when the MC_E is internalized.
   b.   S″ with the same equilibrium P and Q_X when the MC_E is internalized.
   c.   S′ with a different equilibrium P and Q_X when the MC_E is internalized.
   d.   S′ with the same equilibrium P and Q_X when the MC_E is internalized.

CHAPTER 19:

THE ECONOMICS OF INFORMATION

Prior to reading chapter 19, match statements at left with the appropriate concept at right.

___1. Actual outlay of money to acquire inputs

___2. Non-linear production-possibilities frontier

___3. The study of maximization of the benefit-cost of
     individual behaviors

___4. Satisfaction or happiness

___5. Price of one good divided by the price of another

___6. Where transactions between buyers and sellers occur

___7. Extra, additional, or incremental amount

___8. Human factor of production

___9. A change in quantity supplied at each price

___10. Additional revenue from selling one more unit of output

___11. Change in output as one more worker is hired

___12. Additional cost associated with hiring one more worker

___13. Firms that cannot earn normal profits tend to _____

___14. When cartel members attempt to maximize own profits

___15. A commodity for which its consumption by one
      individual does not reduce the amount available
       for others

a. increasing cost

b. labor

c. microeconomics

d. market

e. marginal

f. utility

g. relative price

h. cost

i. marginal product
    of labor

j. exit

k. shift in supply

l. marginal revenue

m. ME

n. public goods

o. cartel cheating
    problem

19.1 THE ECONOMICS OF SEARCH

   A. Search Costs: time spent reading ads, telephoning, traveling, inspecting the product, and comparison shopping for the lowest price

   B. Searching for the Lowest Price: a consumer should continue to search as long as the marginal benefit exceeds the marginal cost. The higher the price of a product and the greater the range of prices, the more searches the consumer will undertake because the marginal benefit is higher

   C. Search and Advertising

     1. **Search goods**: goods whose quality can be evaluated by inspection at the time of purchase

     2. **Experience goods**: goods whose quality cannot be judged by inspection at the time of purchase but only after using them

19.2 ASYMMETRIC INFORMATION: THE MARKET FOR LEMONS AND ADVERSE SELECTION

A. **Asymmetric Information and the Market for Lemons**
1. **Asymmetric information**: one party to a transaction has more information than the other party regarding the quality of the product or service
2. **Adverse selection**: low-quality merchandise drives high-quality merchandise out of the market

B. **The Insurance Market and Adverse Selection**: forces insurance companies to raise rates

19.3 MARKET SIGNALING

The problem of adverse selection resulting from asymmetric information can be resolved or greatly reduced by **market signaling**. If sellers of high-quality products, lower-risk individuals, better-quality borrowers, or more-productive workers can somehow inform or send signals of their superior quality, lower-risk or greater productivity to potential buyers of the products, insurance companies, credit companies, and employers, then the problem of adverse selection can, for the most part, be overcome.

19.4 THE PROBLEM OF MORAL HAZARD

1. **Moral hazard**: increase in the probability of an illness, fire, or other accident when an individual is insured rather then when he or she is not
2. **Coinsurance**: the insurance company will insure only part of the possible loss or value of the property being insured so that the individual or firm shares a significant portion of a potential with the insurance company and will then take more precautions to avoid losses

19.5 THE PRINCIPAL-AGENT PROBLEM

1. **Principal-agent problem**: while owners of a firm want to maximize the total profits or the present value of the firm, the managers or agents want to maximize their own personal interests, such as their salaries, tenure, influence, and reputation
2. **Golden parachutes**: large financial settlements paid out by a firm to its managers if they are forced to leave as a result of the firm being taken over

19.6 THE EFFICIENCY WAGE THEORY

Firms willingly pay higher than equilibrium wages in order to induce workers to avoid shirking or slacking off on the job

---

⌘ AT THE FRONTIER ⌘
THE INTERNET AND THE INFORMATION SUPERHIGHWAY

The goal is to build faster and more sophisticated computers (hardware) and programs (software) for running them and to link them throughout the nation via what has been aptly called an **"information superhighway."** In a more limited sense, a world information superhighway is already here through the **Internet**.

PART III: KEY CONCEPTS IN THIS CHAPTER

1. The time spent reading ads, telephoning, traveling, inspecting the product, and comparative shopping for the lowest price constitutes the _____ cost.
2. The marginal benefit from continuing to searching is greater the _____ the price and the greater the _____ of product prices.
3. Goods whose quality can be evaluated by inspection at the time of purchase are _____ goods, whereas those that cannot be judged by inspection at the time of purchase but only after using them are _____ goods.
4. _____ exists when one party to a transaction has more information than the other party regarding the quality of the product or service.
5. The process of low-quality merchandise driving high-quality merchandise out of the market is called _____. Such a process forces insurance companies to **raise/maintain the same/decrease** rates.
6. The problem of adverse selection that arises from **symmetric/asymmetric** information **can/cannot** be overcome or reduced by the acquisition of more information by the party lacking it.
7. The problem of adverse selection arises in insurance markets when **above-average/below-average** risk people buy insurance, forcing insurance firms to **raise/lower** their premiums.
8. Credit card companies share credit histories of consumers with each other in an attempt to reduce the _____ problem they face.
9. The increase in the probability of an illness, fire, or other accident when an individual is insured than when he or she is not is a _____.
10. Overcoming adverse selection by informing of quality, risk and productivity is _____.
11. The method of _____ used by insurance companies to overcome or reduce the problem of moral hazard compels the individual or firm to share a significant portion of a potential loss with the insurance company, the idea being that the individual or firm will then take precautions to avoid a loss.
12. The problem of _____ arises whenever an externality is present.
13. While owners of a firm want to maximize the total profits or the present value of the firm, the managers want to maximize their own personal interests, such as their salaries, tenure, influence, and reputation. Such a situation is that of the _____.

---

14. The **green bills/golden parachutes/silver linings** are the large financial settlements paid out by a firm to its managers if they are forced to leave as a result of the firm being taken over.
15. The theory that postulates that firms are willing to pay higher than equilibrium wages in order to induce workers to avoid shirking or slacking off on the job is the _____.
16. Economists who work with the efficiency wage models tend to believe that there are solid microeconomic reasons for **sticky/flexible** wages **enabling the market to clear/preventing the market from clearing** automatically.
17. Applying the economic principles of information to job search theory, an unemployed person continues searching for a job as long as the _____ of search is **greater than/equal to/less than** the _____ of search.
18. Applying the economic principles of information to public-choice theory, if the benefits of gathering political information are less than the costs, it **is/is not** economically rational to gather that information. The result is _____.
19. _____ is a government program which covers the elderly, whereas _____ covers the poor.
20. According to the analysis in the text, Medicare and Medicaid have led to a _____ problem.

PART IV: MULTIPLE-CHOICE QUESTIONS

___1. The time spent reading ads, telephoning, traveling, inspecting the product and comparative shopping for the lowest price is called:
   a. down time.
   b. real time.
   c. search costs.
   d. sunk costs.

___2. The most important component of search cost is the:
   a. taxes paid to support government provision of information.
   b. money spent on checking the quality of the product.
   c. time spent learning about the product.
   d. All of the above are equally important.

___3. The case where one party to a transaction has more information than the other party regarding the quality of the product or service is called:
   a. asymmetric information.
   b. perfect knowledge.
   c. symmetric information.
   d. search cost.

___4. When an individual drives more recklessly with automobile insurance than he or she would without the insurance, the insurance industry would identify this as a(n):
   a. ordinary risk.
   b. special risk.
   c. zero risk.
   d. moral hazard.

___5. The problem of adverse selection resulting from asymmetric information can be resolved or greatly reduced by:
   a. coinsurance.
   b. market signaling.
   c. price discrimination.
   d. golden parachutes.

___6. The principal-agent problem is:
   a. a disagreement between a house buyer and a real estate broker.
   b. conflict between the head of a public school and the people who provide services to the school.
   c. due to the separation of ownership from control in modern corporations.
   d. when an agent cannot reach an agreement with an entertainer.

___7. According to the _____ theory, a firm is willing to pay higher than equilibrium wages in order to induce workers not to slack off on the job.
   a. efficiency wage
   b. compensating differences
   c. equal pay for equal work
   d. marginal productivity

___8. Insurance companies use the method of _____ to overcome or reduce the problem of moral hazard:
   a. coinsurance
   b. market signaling
   c. price discrimination
   d. golden parachutes

___9. One way of overcoming the principal-agent problem is to:
   a. provide coinsurance.
   b. engage in arbitrage.
   c. establish golden parachutes.
   d. have government regulation.

___10. In the market for used automobiles, when the end result of market interaction is that low-quality cars drive high-quality cars out of the market, there is:
   a. arbitrage.
   b. adverse selection.
   c. a spot market.
   d. a forward or futures market.

___11. Experience goods are those goods which:
   a. cannot be judged by inspection at the time of purchase but only after using them.
   b. can be judged by inspection at the time of purchase.
   c. have no search costs.
   d. have search costs so high that none can be purchased.

___12. Search goods are those goods which:
   a. cannot be judged by inspection at the time of purchase but only after using them.
   b. can be judged by inspection at the time of purchase.
   c. have no search costs.
   d. have search costs so high that none can be purchased.

___13. The approximate lowest expected price from each additional search for a good is a function of the:
   a. lowest price.
   b. lowest price and the range of possible prices.
   c. lowest price, the range of possible prices, and the number of searches.
   d. expected future prices.

___14. Automobiles, TV sets, and computers are examples of _____ goods.
   a. experience
   b. search
   c. Giffen
   d. public

___15. Fresh fruits and vegetables, apparel, and greeting cards are examples of _____ goods.
   a. experience
   b. search
   c. Giffen
   a. public

___16. Any market characterized by imperfect information has:
   a. externalities.
   b. the problem of adverse selection.
   c. no government regulation.
   d. market signaling.

___17. One method by which insurance companies try to overcome the problem of moral hazard is to:
   a. request government regulation.
   b. specify the precautions that an individual or firm must take as a condition for buying insurance.
   c. require bonding of the individual as a condition for buying insurance.
   d. engage in price discrimination.

___18. By an individual increasing his or her education, there is:
   a. a moral hazard.
   b. coinsurance.
   c. a market signal regarding the productivity of the individual for firms.
   d. asymmetric information.

___19. If the equilibrium wage (w) is $5 per hour, then the efficiency wage is:
   a. higher than $5.
   b. lower than $5.
   c. $5.
   d. either higher than or lower than $5.

___20. The no shirk constraint (NSC) curve is:
   a. a demand curve for labor.
   b. a marginal revenue product (MRP) curve for labor.
   c. a marginal expenditure (ME) curve for labor.
   d. positively sloped.

___21. As a result of asymmetric information in the used car market, owners of "lemons" tend to receive a _____ price than their cars are worth, while owners of high-quality cars receive a _____ price than their cars are worth.
   a. higher, higher
   b. lower, lower
   c. higher, lower
   d. lower, higher

___22. Brand names, chain retailers, and professional licensing reduce:
   a. the degree of asymmetric information.
   b. problem of adverse selection.
   c. the degree of moral hazard.
   d. Both a and b are correct.

___23. If the government were to cover the entire cost of medical services for the poor and the elderly, the:
   a. demand curve (D) for these groups would become more inelastic.
   b. D for these groups would shift left.
   c. D for these groups would shift right.
   d. supply curve for those providing medical services to these groups would shift right.

___24. A firm can signal the higher quality of its products to potential customers by:
   a. adopting brand names, offering guarantees and warranties.
   b. not exchanging defective items.
   c. lowering its price.
   d. raising its price.

___25. One of the ways used by insurance companies to overcome or reduce the problem of moral hazard is:
   a. insuring the entire value of the property.
   b. insuring the entire possible loss.
   c. coinsurance.
   d. price discrimination.

Use Figure 19-1 to answer questions 26 – 30. The figure illustrates the demand for medical services (doctor's visits) by the elderly and the poor before (D_c) and after (D_c') a government subsidy. D_n is the demand curve of the rest of the population.

FIGURE 19-1

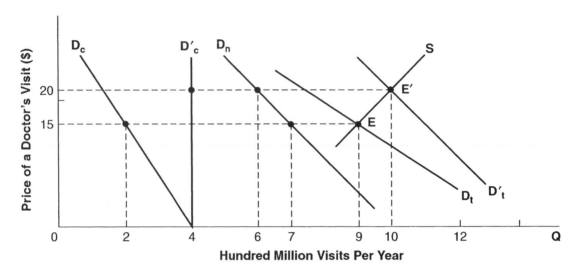

___26. Which of the demand curves represents the total demand for medical services before the government subsidy?
   a. D_t
   b. D_t'
   c. D_n
   d. S

___27. Which of the demand curves represents the total demand for medical services after the government subsidy?
   a. D_t
   b. D_t'
   c. D_n
   d. S

___28. As a result of the government subsidy for the elderly and poor, the price of a doctor's visit for the noncovered group:
   a. rises.
   b. falls.
   c. stays the same.
   d. is the average of the before-subsidy price and the amount of the subsidy.

___29 As a result of the subsidy, the demand for medical services by the poor and elderly has become:
   a. more elastic.
   b. less inelastic.
   c. more inelastic.
   d. Cannot be determined from the information provided.

___30. The moral hazard problem resulting from the government subsidy can be shown as the:
   a. increased demand for doctor's visits by the elderly and poor.
   b. higher price of a doctor's visit to the noncovered group.
   c. greater number of doctor's visits by the elderly and poor.
   d. All of the above are correct.

ANSWERS TO STUDY GUIDE QUESTIONS

ANSWERS FOR CHAPTER 1

Part II: *Key Concepts in this Chapter*

1.scarcity   2. scarce   3. theory   4. markets   5. positive, normative
6. microeconomics   7. opportunity cost   8. normative   9. false
10. macroeconomics   11. hypothesis   12. false   13. Pareto optimum
14. internationalization   15. macroeconomics   16. variables   17. free
18. macroeconomics, positive   19. mixed   20. Marginal

Part III: *Multiple-Choice Questions*

1. D 2. C 3. A 4. B 5. D 6. C 7. B 8. D 9. C 10. A 11. B 12. A 13. C 14. D 15. B 16. A 17. D 18. B 19. C 20. A 21. B 22. D 23. A 24. C 25. D 26. D 27. A 28. B 29. B 30. D

ANSWERS FOR CHAPTER 2

Part I: *Review of Concepts from Earlier Chapter*

1. h 2. e 3. f 4. b 5. g 6. c 7. d 8. A

Part III: *Key Concepts in this Chapter*

1.shortage   2. non-price   3. less, quantity demanded   4. equilibrium
5. comparative static   6. positive   7. shortage   8. downward shift of
9. upward shift of   10. demand, quantity demanded   11. excise tax
12. equilibrium   13. decrease, increase   14. decrease, raising
15. demand for, rise, positive   16. demand for, rise   17. supply of, rises
18. increase, quantity demanded of, a downward shift of

Part IV: *Multiple-Choice Questions*

1. B 2. A 3. C 4. D 5. C 6. D 7. A 8. C 9. A 10. D 11. B 12. C 13. C 14. B 15. B 16. D 17. A 18. A 19. C 20. A 21. B 22. D 23. B 24. B 25. A 26. C 27. B 28. D 29. D 30. B

ANSWERS FOR CHAPTER 3

Part I: *Review of Concepts from Earlier Chapter*

1. a   2. k   3. g   4. i   5. c   6. f   7. b   8. e   9. d   10. h   11. J

Part III: *Key Concepts in this Chapter*

1. utility 2. marginal   3. diminishing, utility, less, more   4. ordinal
5. increase, decrease   6. budget constraint   7. total 8. income
9. marginal, price   10. $100/2 = 50$ 11. $300/5 = 60$
12. meal, meal 13. equal to   14. is 15. greater, A, B, rise, fall   16. flatter
17. neuters   18. intersect 19. marginal utilities   20. are tangent

Part IV: *Multiple-Choice Questions*

1. C 2. A 3. D 4. C 5. B 6. A 7. D 8. B 9. B 10. A 11. A 12. C 13. D 14. D 15. C 16. A 17. B 18. B 19. D 20. C 21. A 22. C 23. C 24. B 25. D 26. D   27. B   28. C 29. D 30. B

ANSWERS FOR CHAPTER 4

Part I: *Review of Concepts from Earlier Chapter*

1. e   2. d   3. b   4. j   5. f   6. g   7. h   8. a   9. i   10. c

Part III: *Key Concepts in this Chapter*

1. in consumer equilibrium   2. income effect   3. consumer's surplus 4. 18
5. 12.5 6. lower, greater   7. marginal   8. Edgeworth box
9. normal   10. substitution   11. Engel   12. Engel
13. income-consumption   14. price-consumption   15. negatively 16. demand
17. Giffen   18. negative 19. negative, decreases, increases   20. Edgeworth box

Part IV: *Multiple-Choice Questions*

1. D 2. C 3. B 4. A 5. A 6. C 7. B 8. C 9. C 10. D 11. D 12. A 13. A 14. C 15. C 16. B 17. D 18. D 19. A 20. A 21. B 22. C 23. C 24. B 25. D 26. C 27. A 28. B 29. D 30. A

ANSWERS FOR CHAPTER 5

Part I: *Review of Concepts from Earlier Chapter*

1. a 2. g 3. b 4. c 5. h 6. f 7. d 8. e

Part III: *Key Concepts in this Chapter*

1. consumers 2. elastic, inelastic 3. rise, more than 4. fall, less than
5. one, unitary elastic 6. less than, decrease 7. fall, larger, fall
8. substitutes, time 9. larger, smaller 10. greater 11. larger
12. few, decrease 13. complements, negative 14. substitutes, positive
15. 7.5% less, inferior 16. 9% more, normal 17. cross 18. substitute
19. income elasticity 20. inferior

Part IV: *Multiple-Choice Questions*

1. D 2. A 3. C 4. B 5. A 6. A 7. A 8. B 9. B 10. C 11. C 12. C 13. A 14. B 15. D 16. C 17. B 18. A 19. B 20. D 21. D 22. C 23. D 24. A 25. C 26. B 27. D 28. C 29. A 30. A

ANSWERS FOR CHAPTER 6

Part I: *Review of Concepts from Earlier Chapter*

1. c 2. e 3. d 4. b 5. f 6. h 7. i 8. l 9. k 10. g 11. a 12. j

Part III: *Key Concepts in this Chapter*

1. certainty 2. risk 3. uncertainty 4. risk 5. strategy 6. standard deviation
7. averters 8. averters, diminishing 9. expected utility 10. averter
11. true 12. positively 13. steeper 14. purchasing insurance
15. diversification 16. negative 17. risk 18. equal to

19. forward, futures   20. true

Part IV: *Multiple-Choice Questions*

1. A 2. B 3. C 4. C 5. A 6. D 7. C 8. A 9. B 10. C 11. A 12. C 13. A 14. D 15. C 16. B 17. A 18. C 19. C 20. C 21. A 22. B 23. A 24. D 25. A 26. B   27. B   28. D 29. C 30. D

ANSWERS FOR CHAPTER 7

Part I: *Review of Concepts from Earlier Chapter*

1. c   2. j   3. h   4. i   5. f   6. b   7. d   8. e   9. g   10. a

Part III: *Key Concepts in this Chapter*

1.fixed inputs 2. production function 3. marginal product   4. diminishing returns
5. isoquants   6. upward 7. input prices, marginal products
8. negatively, convex, do not   9. marginal rate of technical substitution
10. is not, returns, scale 11. increasing returns, long run   12. technological progress, process innovation   13. product cycle   14. constant 15. marginal products
16. fixed-proportions 17. greater   18. positively 19. closer together 20. constant

Part IV: *Multiple-Choice Questions*

1. C 2. B 3. A 4. D 5. C 6. B 7. C 8. A 9. C 10. D 11. A 12. A 13. D 14. C 15. B 16. C 17. D 18. B 19. C 20. A 21. C 22. D 23. C 24. C 25. D 26. A   27. C 28. C 29. D 30. C

ANSWERS FOR CHAPTER 8

Part I: *Review of Concepts from Earlier Chapter*

1. g   2. b   3. a   4. d   5. h   6. c   7. f   8. e   9. i   10. m 11. j
12. l   13. k

Part III: *Key Concepts in this Chapter*

1.explicit   2. isocost   3. least-cost   4. fixed, fixed   5. variable, variable   6. fixed, variable, fixed, variable 7. variable   8. marginal   9. diminishing, inversely
10. variable, output 11. decreasing, increasing 12. minimum   13. $20.00, fixed   14. short, long, expansion, long 15. average, marginal 16. average cost, average
17. increasing 18. scope   19. learning curve   20. minimum efficient scale (MES)

Part IV: *Multiple-Choice Questions*

1. C 2. A 3. D 4. C 5. C 6. B 7. A 8. D 9. C 10. D 11. B 12. D 13. A 14. A 15. C 16. D 17. C 18. B 19. A 20. B 21. B 22. D 23. C 24. A 25. D26. B   27. A 28. C 29. D 30. C

ANSWERS FOR CHAPTER 9

Part I: *Review of Concepts from Earlier Chapter*

1. f   2. h   3. k   4. a   5. c   6. e   7. d   8. i   9. b   10. g   11. j
12. m   13. l

Part III: *Key Concepts in this Chapter*

1. many, small, takers   2. homogeneous, mobility, perfect knowledge   3. market
4. profits, break-even   5. marginal revenue, marginal cost, average variable cost
6. all of the above   7. large, elastic, horizontal   8. marginal cost 9. all of the above
10. none of the above   11. 1000, 900, 300, 100   12. 10, 10, impossible to determine
13. keep constant   14. market supply   15. entry, supply, price, long
16. zero, all of the above   17. increasing 18. decreasing, downward
19. fall, external   20. efficiency, intersects

Part IV: *Multiple-Choice Questions*

1. D 2. A 3. C 4. B 5. C 6. C 7. C 8. D 9. B 10. A 11. D 12. A 13. A 14. C 15. D 16. D 17. C 18. B 19. A 20. B 21. C 22. D 23. B 24. A 25. A26. C   27. A 28. B 29. C 30. B

ANSWERS FOR CHAPTER 10

Part I: *Review of Concepts from Earlier Chapter*

1. g 2. j 3. f 4. a 5. k 6. l 7. e 8. i 9. c 10. b 11. h
12. d 13. n 14. m

Part III: *Key Concepts in this Chapter*

1. pure monopoly   2. natural monopoly   3. market, is not   4. less, below
5. does not guarantee   6. 112, 7, 14, higher   7. cannot, unique
8. marginal revenue, long-run marginal cost   9. MR, MC, exceeds 10. loss
11. higher, smaller   12. marginal cost, marginal revenue
13. equal sized, SAC, SMC, LAC, LMC 14. price discrimination   15. 3, first
16. third, necessary   17. second   18. dumping   19. bundling
20. perfectly competitive, monopolistic

Part IV: *Multiple-Choice Questions*

1. A 2. D 3. B 4. C 5. D 6. B 7. C 8. A 9. A 10. C 11. D 12. D 13. B 14. B 15. C 16.
D 17. C 18. B 19. B 20. A 21. A 22. C 23. D 24. B 25. C 26. D 27. A 28. C 29. C
30. C

ANSWERS FOR CHAPTER 11

Part I: *Review of Concepts from Earlier Chapter*

1. j 2. e 3. l 4. b 5. d 6. h 7. m 8. k 9. f 10. g 11. c
12. a 13. i 14. p 15. o 16. n

Part III: *Key Concepts in this Chapter*

1. many, heterogeneous, differentiated, easy   2. differentiated, group
3. searcher, exceeds, elastic   4. exceeds, distributive (or allocative) 5. Excess capacity 6.
product variation   7. oligopoly, searchers 8. concentration ratio, lower
9. are several theories, interdependence 10. Cournot model, Bertrand
11. does not, contrary to   12. kinked demand curve, loses, loses   13. collusion, cartel
14. centralized cartel, market-sharing cartel   15. price leadership, barometric firm
16. limit pricing   17. non-price competition   18. does not, LAC, can, greater, beyond
19. cost-plus pricing   20. global oligopolists, internal, mergers, banking

---

Part IV: *Multiple-Choice Questions*

1. D 2. A 3. C 4. B 5. B 6. A 7. C 8. D 9. C 10. B 11. A 12. A 13. D 14. C 15. D 16. B 17. A 18. A 19. B 20. C 21. C 22. D 23. B 24. C 25. D 26. D 27. A 28. B 29. C 30. B

ANSWERS FOR CHAPTER 12

Part I: *Review of Concepts from Earlier Chapter*

1. f 2. d 3. i 4. c 5. a 6. b 7. h 8. e 9. g 10. k 11. m 12. m 13. j 14. l 15. o

Part III: *Key Concepts in this Chapter*

1. game 2. players 3. strategies, sales, profitability 4. strategies, payoffs
5. payoff matrix 6. dominant strategy, Nash equilibrium 7. prisoner's dilemma
8. cooperative 9. dominant 10. repeated, tit-for-tat 11. tit-for-tat 12. strategic move
13. entry deterrence 14. competitive advantage 15. prisoner's dilemma 16. outcome
17. payoff matrix 18. Nash equilibrium 19. confesses, does not confess
20. the payoff of one player, the payoff of the second player

Part IV: *Multiple-Choice Questions*

1. A 2. C 3. C 4. D 5. D 6. C 7. A 8. A 9. B 10. D 11. A 12. C 13. B 14. A 15. C 16. D 17. C 18. B 19. B 20. A 21. B 22. C 23. D 24. B 25. C 26. D 27. A 28. A 29. C 30. D

ANSWERS FOR CHAPTER 13

Part I: *Review of Concepts from Earlier Chapter*

1. c 2. e 3. d 4. b 5. f 6. i 7. h 8. j 9. m 10. l 11. g 12. a 13. k 14. o 15. n

Part III: *Key Concepts in this Chapter*

1. efficiency, marginal cost   2. Herfindahl index   3. contestable markets
4. Lerner index   5. experimental economics   6. Sherman Act, 1890
7. illegal, trade, commerce 8. conscious parallelism 9. mergers 10. 10,000
11. larger 12. natural monopoly, public utilities   13. Averch-Johnson
14. voluntary export restraints (VERs) 15. SAC, SMC 16. higher, higher
17. transfer pricing   18. below, loss   19. zero   20. 1970s, deregulation

Part IV: *Multiple-Choice Questions*

1. C 2. A 3. A 4. D 5. D 6. A 7. A 8. C 9. B 10. B 11. D 12. D 13. A 14. C 15. B 16. C 17. D 18. A 19. A 20. B 21. C 22. D 23. B 24. B 25. D 26. C 27. A 28. C 29. B 30. C

ANSWERS FOR CHAPTER 14

Part I: *Review of Concepts from Earlier Chapter*

1. f 2. d 3. i 4. c 5. a 6. b 7. h 8. e 9. g 10. k 11. m
12. n 13. j 14. l 15. o

Part III: *Key Concepts in this Chapter*

1. derived   2. income, marginal product, marginal revenue   3. 7, $77
4. $11, $11, is not, horizontal   5. $11, equals   6. price, equals
7. extra, input, total cost, quantity of input hired
8. $50, remains the same, taker 9. horizontal, supply, $50
10. greater, equals 11. downward, diminishing 12. complementary
13. substitutes 14. substitutes, demand, supply, cost
15. substitution, income, opposite   16. marginal productivity
17. mobile, equalization   18. economic rent   19. non-competing groups
20. unemployment gap, disemployment

Part IV: *Multiple-Choice Questions*

1. B 2. A 3. C 4. A 5. D 6. C 7. C 8. B 9. A 10. C 11. D 12. B 13. A 14. C 15. B 16. B 17. D 18. C 19. B 20. A 21. C 22. A 23. C 24. B 25. C 26. D 27. B 28. C 29. C 30. D

ANSWERS FOR CHAPTER 15

Part I: *Review of Concepts from Earlier Chapter*

1. i 2. n 3. m 4. j 5. a 6. c 7. b 8. k 9. f 10. l 11. g
12. h 13. o 14. d 15. e

Part III: *Key Concepts in this Chapter*

1. marginal cost, marginal revenue, labor, MP, capital, MP 2. marginal revenue product
3. monopolistic exploitation 4. MRP, movement along, shift, right, substitutes
5. horizontal, summation 6. similarly to, perfectly competitive 7. monopsony
8. fewer, ceteris paribus, rise, inelastic 9. more
10. oligopsony, monopsonistic competition 11. monopsonistic exploitation
12. marginal cost, marginal revenue, MRP, MP, MRP, MP
13. brain drain 14. marginal revenue product, supply 15. bilateral
16. labor union, oppose 17. unionized, lower
18. restricting, above, increasing 19. more 20. discrimination

Part IV: *Multiple-Choice Questions*

1. C 2. A 3. D 4. B 5. A 6. C 7. D 8. A 9. A 10. B 11. C 12. B 13. D 14. C 15. B 16.
B 17. A 18. A 19. D 20. D 21. C 22. B 23. A 24. C 25. B 26. D 27. B 28. D 29. B
30. C

ANSWERS FOR CHAPTER 16

Part I: *Review of Concepts from Earlier Chapter*

1. g 2. d 3. k 4. c 5. l 6. a 7. i 8. m 9. e 10. j 11. b
12. h 13. f 14. o 15. n

Part III: *Key Concepts in this Chapter*

1. endowment position, wealth 2. rate, interest, equilibrium
3. capital budgeting, net present value 4. separate, separation
5. default, variability, default risk, variability risk 6. real, real, real, nominal
7. cost, equity capital, cost, debt 8. 85.73, should not
9. 89, should, increases 10. 683,013.46 11. 4 12. $654,000

13. should, positive   14. $21.60   15. $24,800   16. 7%
17. capital asset pricing   18. beta coefficient   19. reduce, increase
20. greater than

Part IV: *Multiple-Choice Questions*

1. B 2. A 3. D 4. C 5. A 6. B 7. C 8. C 9. A 10. D 11. B 12. B 13. C 14. D 15. D 16. A 17. B 18. B 19. C 20. C 21. A 22. D 23. B 24. D 25. C 26. A 27. B 28. D 29. C 30. D

ANSWERS FOR CHAPTER 17

Part I: *Review of Concepts from Earlier Chapter*

1. g   2. d   3. k   4. c   5. l   6. a   7. i   8. m   9. e   10. j   11. b
12. h   13. f   14. o   15. n

Part III: *Key Concepts in this Chapter*

1. partial equilibrium   2. interdependence, general equilibrium
3. contract curve, exchange   4. contract curve, production
5. production-possibilities frontier 6. marginal rate, transformation
7. Edgeworth box, exchange, Edgeworth box, production
8. marginal rate of transformation, equal to, marginal rate of substitution
9. economic efficiency 10. Pareto optimality   11. invisible hand   12. welfare
13. two, Pareto optimal, convex, competitive equilibrium
14. imperfect competition, externalities, public goods
15. utility-possibilities 16. grand utility-possibilities
17. comparative advantage 18. favor of, harms, benefits
19. Arrow's impossibility theorem   20. Kaldor-Hicks

Part IV: *Multiple-Choice Questions*

1. A 2. C 3. B 4. B 5. D 6. D 7. C 8. B 9. A 10. A 11. D 12. B 13. B 14. C 15. A 16. C 17. B 18. D 19. D 20. B 21. A 22. C 23. A 24. B 25. D 26. D 27. B 28. C 29. A 30. B

ANSWERS FOR CHAPTER 18

Part I: *Review of Concepts from Earlier Chapter*

1. h   2. a   3. c   4. f   5. g   6. d   7. e   8. b   9. k   10. l   11. i
12. m   13. j   14. o   15. n

Part III: *Key Concepts in this Chapter*

1. externalities, positive, external, negative, external
2. external diseconomies of production, external diseconomies of consumption
3. external economies of production, external economies of consumption
4. technical externalities, monopoly, exceeds   5. common, common, overgrazed, is not   6.
Coase, zero, regardless   7. Coase, internalize   8. internalizing, transferable
9. public, simultaneously, nonrival   10. is, is not, is, is not   11. nonexclusion
12. free riders   13. benefit-cost analysis   14. political   15. government failures
16. lower, rational ignorance   17. special-interest groups, strong
18. bureaucrats, unelected, more, interest group members have
19. marginal benefit, marginal cost   20. effluent fee

Part IV: *Multiple-Choice Questions*

1. D 2. A 3. C 4. A 5. C 6. D 7. A 8. C 9. D 10. B 11. A 12. A 13. D 14. C 15. D 16.
B 17. A 18. C 19. D 20. C 21. A 22. B 23. C 24. D 25. A 26. A   27. B 28. C 29. A
30. B

ANSWERS FOR CHAPTER 19

Part I: *Review of Concepts from Earlier Chapter*

1. h   2. a   3. c   4. f   5. g   6. d   7. e   8. b   9. k   10. l   11. i
12. m   13. j   14. o   15. n

Part III: *Key Concepts in this Chapter*

1. search   2. higher, range   3. search, experience   4. asymmetric information
5. adverse selection, raise   6. asymmetric, can   7. above-average, raise
8. adverse selection   9. moral hazard   10. market signaling   11. coinsurance
12. moral hazard   13. principal-agent problem   14. golden parachutes
15. efficiency wage theory   16. sticky, preventing the market from clearing

17. benefit, greater than, cost   18. is not, rational ignorance 19. Medicare, Medicaid
20. moral hazard

Part IV: *Multiple-Choice Questions*

1. C 2. C 3. A 4. D 5. B 6. C 7. A 8. A 9. C 10. B 11. A 12. B 13. C 14. A 15. B 16.
B 17. B 18. C 19. A 20. D 21. C 22. D 23. C 24. A 25. C 26. A   27. B 28. A 29. C
30. D